ENDORSEMENTS

Steven has written a book in which every page is the developing process for a faith algorithm.

It will sustain you and at the same time inspire you to challenge yourself to live and achieve the dreams and desires you thought would never come to pass. You will read this book, chapter by chapter, many times over.

LLOYD BUSTARD
Founder and Lead Pastor of World Worship Center
www.worldworshipchurch.org

Throughout the years of friendship that I have shared with Pastor Steven, his cheerful demeanor has never failed to exhibit the essence of genuine faith—a posture of confident expectation and consistent hope in the integrity of God's Word.

Faith is based on a personal relationship, not on a rigid formula. The foundations of Pastor Steven's faith are rooted in his fasted lifestyle and his diligence in practicing watchful prayer even in the wee hours of the morning. These foundations have anchored him throughout these years, and have formed the basis of his many adventures of faith in Christ.

Manifesting the Blessings of God offers practical gems gleaned from the personal experiences of this beloved prophet. Through expounding upon faith's trials and triumphs, it teaches precious lessons concerning the dynamic workings of faith. The triumphant testimonies detailed in the book affirm that faith in God guarantees success and excellence in every area of one's endeavors. Faith is a trustful leap out of the unknown and into the known will of God; until you lay hold of kingdom faith, life will remain a perpetual struggle.

Steadfast faith planted in the soil of patient trust in God will yield a bountiful harvest of victories. Patience is a powerful ally of faith; in fact, it is so important that it was mentioned thirty-two times throughout the New Testament. There is no doubt that the powerful duo of faith and patience will always yield miraculous breakthroughs (see Heb. 6:12,15).

Just as many have been blessed by his insightful teachings all across the world, I believe that you too will receive revelations through this book that will propel you to a higher level of spiritual development. Friends, firmly grasp the reins of faith, for it is your turn to reign!

DR. JEDIDIAH THAM
Living Lilies
www.livinglilies.org

I have read a great book, a very great book. It seems to me that Steven is going to help each disciple of Jesus to deepen his spiritual life, his prayer life, and his life of intimacy with God. What else could I ask? I wish, from the bottom of my heart, that even unbelievers may read this book because each soul is thirsty to meet the living God. May God bless the readers and His author.

FATHER GEOFFROY DE LESTRANGE
Priest of Sante Julie Billiart du Ressontois
www.paroissecatholique.ressons.info

Manifesting the
BLESSINGS
of GOD

DESTINY IMAGE BOOKS BY STEVEN BROOKS

Working with Angels

How to Operate in the Gifts of the Spirit

Standing on the Shoulders of Giants

Fasting and Prayer

The Sacred Anointing

Manifesting the
BLESSINGS
of GOD

HOW TO RECEIVE EVERY PROMISE AND PROVISION
THAT HEAVEN HAS MADE AVAILABLE

STEVEN BROOKS

DESTINY IMAGE® PUBLISHERS, INC.
P.O. Box 310, Shippensburg, PA 17257-0310
"Promoting Inspired Lives."

This book and all other Destiny Image and Destiny Image Fiction books are available at Christian bookstores and distributors worldwide.

Cover design by Eileen Rockwell
Interior design by Terry Clifton

For more information on foreign distributors, call 717-532-3040.

Reach us on the Internet: www.destinyimage.com.

ISBN 13 TP: 978-0-7684-1076-1
ISBN 13 eBook: 978-0-7684-1077-8
LP ISBN: 978-0-7684-1472-1
HC ISBN: 978-0-7684-1473-8

For Worldwide Distribution, Printed in the U.S.A.
2 3 4 5 6 7 8 / 21 20 19 18 17

DEDICATION

This book is dedicated to Kelly, my wife. She has been with me all the way through this exciting journey of faith. Together we have traveled the world ministering the gospel, and we have seen the goodness of God at every turn. She is the joy of my life and I'm grateful to God that she and I can live each day experiencing the new wonders and adventures that await us. Whether it's a new meeting to minister in, a new restaurant to try, or a tucked-away coffeehouse, we truly enjoy every moment of time we have. We are eager to embrace our next decade of laughter and discovery with one another!

ACKNOWLEDGMENTS

The world has come a long way in making various technological advances. No longer do we have to write on scrolls of parchment with a feathered quill. Although I had long left behind writing my manuscripts on paper with ink, I did find myself typing with an outdated laptop. Over time several keys began to come loose, making it difficult to type when the "A" key and "W" key were pressed. My laptop was seven years old and I felt that it needed to be retired; perhaps it could be placed in a museum next to a dinosaur exhibit, somewhere where it would be age appropriate. After pressing through several computer glitches I knew it was time to call it a wrap when the dreaded "blue screen" appeared. Although I resuscitated my computer after several attempts to save all data, the writing was on the wall. The book you now hold in your hands was created on my brand-new Apple laptop, which was graciously provided by my Covenant Ministry Partners. They delight in helping me tackle special ministry projects—whether it's a new laptop or a major moon-shot project, they are always willing to contribute. Kudos to them, and the deepest appreciation as they also share in the eternal rewards that come out of this book.

CONTENTS

FOREWORD

I'm quite impressed with how Pastor Steven Brooks launches you into the faith realm of receiving blessings and miracles with his fresh insights into scriptural principles.

When I read his stories illustrating how faith must have its corresponding works or it is dead, I remembered how he planted a valuable watch into my life when he requested my apostolic prayers for three of his properties to sell. He wanted to launch a television studio and ministry. God rewarded his faith (with its action) by selling those properties.

Do you want to learn God's secrets for divine connections, open doors, biblical prosperity, and blessings that chase you and overtake you? This book will inspire you to hear the Holy Spirit and flow in continual miraculous blessings.

This book could change your life because God's blessings are so important to every believer but often are not being appropriated.

Your Father, God, wants you blessed! The first act of God after He created Adam and Eve was to speak a blessing over them (see Gen. 1:22).

The first act God performed in relating to each of His patriarchs (Abraham, Isaac, Jacob) was to speak a blessing over them.

The last act Moses performed before departing from this earth was to bring together the heads of the twelve tribes of Israel and impart blessings to each of them.

Jesus' first ministry to His twelve disciples after gathering them together was to speak a series of blessings over them (see the Beatitudes found in Matthew 5:3–12).

In Luke 24:50-51, the last act of Jesus while He was ascending into the heavens was to bless His disciples!

I believe Pastor Steven Brooks has written this book knowing God's blessing has to be extremely important if everything in our relationship with Him on this earth begins and ends with His blessings!

Why do so many of God's children have low self-esteem, insecurities, poor relationships, and emotional strongholds? They don't know how to appropriate and manifest the blessing of God!

I love the great stories Pastor Steven shares throughout this book that illustrate how being led by God's Spirit, acting on God's principles, and stepping out in faith and action will release God's kingdom, the angelic realm, and the continual blessings of God in your life.

Pastor Steven's creative ideas and implementations of biblical principles will jumpstart the creativity and witty inventions God wants you to move in. He even has a chapter describing "Nine Keys to Unlocking a Heart's Desire Vehicle." I've always placed scriptures and pictures on my refrigerator of what I'm believing for (see Hab. 2:2), so I fully relate to his faith keys. All my close friends know I always believe for and receive what's on my fridge. Anointed men like Kenneth Hagin, Gordon Lindsay, and John G. Lake have inspired my faith in years past. I'm adding Steven Brooks to that list of faith champions!

Dr. Gary Greenwald
Eagles' Nest Ministries
eaglesnestministries.org

Chapter One

THE REVELATION OF FAITH

Faith is one of the greatest assets we have as believers in Christ. An unlimited number of possibilities can be accomplished when we use our faith. In this regard, faith is similar to water in its enduring value. With water we can wash our clothes, quench our thirst, clean our vehicles, water our lawns, or even brush our teeth. Faith has the ability to accomplish multifaceted goals, dreams, and visions. You have to drink water to stay alive. You have to use your faith to receive Jesus, who is the water of eternal life. Through faith you receive salvation, the infilling of the Holy Spirit, healing, prosperity, and miraculous answers to prayer. Faith is so vital that without it you simply cannot please God.

When I grew up, as a young boy I remember that we always went to church every time the doors were opened. We were there consistently every Sunday morning, Sunday night, Wednesday night, and also for special meetings that fell at other times. My parents taught my brothers and me to serve the Lord from an early age and onward. In each meeting the preacher would teach from the Bible, and he covered the various books of the Bible, especially the New Testament. The messages were delivered in a nonemotional type presentation with an emphasis on facts and overall basic knowledge of the Word of God.

Yet when I grew into adulthood and started working full time, I discovered that most of those messages could not help me answer certain problems that I was encountering in life.

I am eternally thankful that I was raised in a Christian home and learned the Bible when I was young. By the age of eight every child in the church could name all of the books in the New Testament in order. By the age of twelve many could name all of the books in the entire Bible, both Old and New Testaments, in order. Some could even quote all the books in the Bible not only forward but also backward! We had great knowledge of the Word of God, but we did not understand how to believe God for specific promises that are found in the Bible. For most Christians who are well versed in the basic knowledge of God's Word, it is important to realize that the devil will not contend with you over basic issues. However, the devil will oppose you over promises that are specifically directed to you from God's Word by the Holy Spirit.

As a child of God it is important to know the devil will not waste his time endeavoring to get you to doubt that Jonah was swallowed by a large fish. You have read the story before and you know it's in the Bible, therefore it's the holy Word of God and you receive it as truth. You have no doubt that Jonah spent three days and three nights in the belly of a large fish. It's the same situation with the Red Sea crossing. The waters of the Red Sea were parted and the Israelites crossed over on dry ground. The Egyptians attempted to do the same thing but the waters crashed in upon them and Pharaoh's army drowned. As believers we have no doubt concerning these epic events that have become known to the whole world. As fantastic and miraculous as these stories are, this is not the area that the devil will try to oppose you. However, the moment you step out in faith to believe that God will do a specific miracle for you is when you discover the enemy's adversarial forces.

The devil doesn't mind if you learn to read the New Testament in the original Greek language. He also doesn't care if you learn to read the Old Testament in the original Hebrew. These specific skills may be required for those who teach in seminaries or universities, and in essence they can be very helpful in biblical studies. But this type of knowledge still isn't enough to produce victory. The enemy is not afraid of head knowledge. After all, the devil himself is clever at quoting Scripture (out of context), which we see when he tempted Jesus during His forty days of prayer and fasting in the desert. The blessings of God are manifested through the process of learning to exercise faith through the living Word of God that is spoken to you. The enemy labors to block God's people from receiving the revelation of faith. A revelation is an unveiling—a pulling back of a curtain to see what has been there all the time. The revelation of faith comes when you realize the power and unlimited possibilities contained within the statement that Jesus made, saying, "all things are possible to him who believes" (Mark 9:23). Through faith you access not just one, but all of the promises of God.

My Christian upbringing was invaluable. The story of redemption was clearly explained to me at an early age. During the pre-church Sunday school class for children, I can still remember learning of David and his battle with Goliath, Noah's ark, Gideon, and countless other stories in the Bible. As I grew up, I eventually came to understand the message of salvation—that Christ died for my sins and that I could receive forgiveness and eternal life through His shed blood. Through faith I received Christ as my Lord and Savior and was baptized as a senior in high school.

Once I was saved, it never occurred to me that I could use my faith for anything else. Most of the sermons that were preached in my home church were evangelistic. Even if there were no visitors or unsaved people in the meetings the pastor would still almost always preach a message about salvation, even though we were all saved. In essence, we really didn't know what to do with our faith after we had been born again. Because we didn't know what to do with it, we therefore did nothing with it. This led to an inability to find success and fulfillment in life as a Christian.

I was raised in a mainline denominational church that staunchly did not believe in modern-day miracles. Speaking in tongues and all forms of the supernatural gifts of God were explained to us by our pastor as having ceased when the last of the first-century apostles died. No clear explanation of this belief was ever fully provided and you were never encouraged to ask. We were also taught that to use musical instruments such as a piano or an acoustic guitar in worship was an act of the devil. With grave instructions spoken in somber tones we were warned that to use them in any worship service would certainly send a person to hell when they died. We were sternly informed that the poor soul who committed the much greater sin of playing more advanced instruments of unrighteousness such as the electric guitar or drums in church would receive a greater punishment in a hotter section of hell, and such people were to be considered reprobate and forever lost.

In order to keep it safe and skip out on being sent to the lake of fire for the sake of some great-sounding guitar riffs, we sang all of our worship songs acapella (without musical instruments). No clapping was ever allowed because we believed it might remind God of those "evil drums" that the preacher referred to. Even despite never having musical instruments in church and being under a form of heavy legalism that suppressed emotion and even restricted the act of lifting ones hands, there was still an inner joy that would arise during our times of singing because some of the songs we sang truly glorified the Lord and we sang them with sincerity from our hearts. The grace of God can also sneak in through the most unexpected ways, even in places of strangling legalism.

Although we did not have the blessing of worshiping with musical instruments, we all learned over time to sing in four-part harmony without being taught how to do it. Even those with voices that were not musically gifted could still sing in tune, and almost every person could read the musical notes from the song books. In some ways we can miss out in our modern worship when we let the worship team carry the whole worship service. Sometimes the sound from the musical instruments can be so loud that you can't even hear the voice of the congregation. Often today, many Christians in church don't sing but just clap along and enjoy the beat of the music. But God wants each individual to worship Him. He wants you to sing to Him from your heart, and He desires for the whole congregation to be united as one voice in worship. It is this corporate unity that causes God to inhabit the praises of His people.

After high school, I headed off to college in fulfillment of my parent's wishes for me to "gain an education." Plunging myself thousands of dollars into debt through federally granted student loans (which took over twenty years to pay back) I found myself having fun in college but also bored. While college can be an excellent choice for some young men and women, I can look back and see that it wasn't God's plan for me. But at that time I couldn't discern the will of God because I didn't have an established prayer life and my mind was not being daily renewed with the Word of God. Although I went to college for four years and did well in track and field as a middle distance runner and earned various athletic honors, I finished my time there with a grade point average that was lower than the required minimum to graduate.

At this point I decided to transfer to a different college and raise my GPA to earn my bachelor's degree. Despite not achieving academic success due to lack of vision and poor choices, I did begin to develop a deep and growing desire to know God and serve Him. It was at this stage of my life that God's plan for me would begin to escalate by His marvelous grace.

The Bible tells us that faith comes by hearing, and hearing by the word of God. At the age of twenty-two, the Lord prepped me to receive one of His greatest blessings—the baptism in the Holy Spirit—by leading me to listen to a preacher on the radio whom I came to love; his name was R.W. Schambach. His preaching intrigued me because he seemed to have a fire in his messages that I never heard in any of our denominational preachers when they preached. Having just moved to a new city and enrolled in a large university in an effort to complete my college degree, I took a part-time job pruning apple trees. This work extended through the entire summer and into the fall, and it was while picking and pruning apples that I discovered Brother Schambach on the radio.

As I listened to him daily on the radio for almost a year I began to realize he was the type of preacher I had been warned about when growing up—he was a Pentecostal preacher. We had been told to steer clear of the Pentecostals because it was said they spoke in tongues and swung from the chandeliers in church. But I could clearly notice an unusual power in Brother Schambach's preaching that mystified me. Finally, after listening to his fifteen-minute radio message each afternoon, Monday through Friday, every week for a year, I became convinced that God still performed miracles. Faith from hearing all of those messages had risen in my heart to receive a blessing from God.

At this same time, I began visiting a small Charismatic church just across the main street from the university entrance. It was in this church that I was filled with the Holy Spirit and first spoke in tongues when the pastor laid his hands on me and prayed, asking God to fill me with the Holy Spirit. Now my faith was moving forward. I had used my faith to receive salvation. Now through faith I had obtained the baptism in the Holy Spirit with the evidence of speaking in tongues. It began to dawn on me that perhaps I could also use my faith for other needs and desires as well. Once again, God had a blessing in store for me through another radio minister.

Whenever you live in a city for a year or two you eventually will discover who's on the radio. This was before the boon of cable and satellite television networks and even satellite radio, so more people listened to the local radio stations back then. There was a Christian FM radio station in the city, and I already was aware of who came on at the various time slots throughout the day. This radio station featured primarily Bible teachers from the various streams of Christianity. There was a certain minister who was on the radio every day whom I had listened to a few times before, but I could never understand anything he was saying. But after I was filled with the Holy Spirit I heard him on the radio, and I completely understood clearly the message he was teaching. It's like a veil was lifted off the eyes of my understanding. The minister was Kenneth E. Hagin, and his teaching on faith would begin to supply me with the spiritual resources I needed to begin to win in life. The change came slowly, very slowly because I had so many layers of religious indoctrination ingrained into me. I felt like an onion that was being peeled, one layer at a time, of a wrong mind-set concerning who God was. The truth of His goodness was gradually unfolding before me.

And you shall know the truth, and the truth shall make you free (John 8:32).

Truth that remains undiscovered can't empower you to new levels of freedom; rather, it is the truth you comprehend that supplies access to new possibilities of extraordinary living. Your faith in God is going to take you into realms that you never knew were possible.

Many Christians have lived in a type of survival mode, simply existing but never crossing over in a tangible way to the place of their blessings in Christ being manifested. When this occurs it can become easy to settle far below God's intended desire of blessing. The difficulties, discouragement, and the need to swim upstream in a prevailing downstream current can be fatiguing. Because of these consistent detrimental conditions, many believers don't reach their destination of seeing their hopes and dreams materialized. Instead of winning in life they are defeated by the world, the flesh, the devil, or by all three at the same time. However, faith in God can turn any situation around, but faith must come by revelation. When you are filled with the Holy Spirit and speak in tongues and also study God's Word, then new levels of revelation begin to break forth in your spirit just like the breaking forth of light.

When you know God's Word you will also begin to discern His will for your life. Then you can take the promises of God by faith and make them evident in the natural realm so that your needs and desires can be met. As you study the pages of this book, expect the Lord to grant you a deeper revelation of faith. Any unfulfilled prophecies, unaccomplished dreams, unexecuted promises, or ingenious ideas yet undischarged need to be reexamined in light of faith and its vast potential. You will see that all things are possible to him who believes. Believes what? Believes what the Word says and what the Holy Spirit speaks to you. The Holy Spirit will speak and reveal the word of the Lord to you. The promise of that specific word will produce much joy in your life when it is manifested. This is why we need to be strong in faith. So that our lives glorify God and we manifest the promises of God.

The earth and the people therein are still waiting to see the manifestation of the sons of God. They do not want to be told an *explanation* of the sons of God, but because they are naturally minded they must see the *manifestation* and proofs of what it is we declare. You may be able to explain something that you believe quite well, but you can only show to others what you have manifested. My prayer is that as you read these pages your faith will break loose to go out and bring into manifestation the promises that God has spoken to you. This will bring much glory to God, it will be a witness to those in the world, it will inspire the church, and it will bring happy fulfillment and lasting joy into the depths of your heart.

Chapter Two

ASKING FOR AND RECEIVING DESIRES

*If you abide in Me, and My words abide in you, you
will ask what you desire, and it shall be done for you.*
—JOHN 15:7

According to the words of Jesus, two conditions required for the
manifestation of personal desires are outlined in the above Scripture.
These two conditions are that we must abide in Christ, and His words
must abide in us.

Abiding in Christ speaks of having a strong devotional life where
the presence of God is maintained in our daily activities. This is not
easy to do, but it is possible for every believer to achieve. It takes much
diligence on our part to keep the Lord as our continual greatest pursuit and priority.

The words of Jesus must always be fresh in our mind. There are
so many things that compete for our mental attention. The world has
become more brazen and shocking. Heinous and violent acts that were
once rare in occurrence have now become commonplace. To keep the

words of Christ at the forefront of our minds requires us to put more of His words in as compared to the other things we absorb.

For instance, if you watch two hours of news at night before going to bed then you will go to sleep with the news having the dominant influence upon your thought life. Saying a ten-minute prayer before falling asleep or reading your Bible for ten minutes in a drowsy condition is not enough to counteract the previous two hours of news that contained reports of financial uncertainty, terror, murder, violence, and endless pharmaceutical commercials. Yet this is the way in which many Christians live, and then when they ask God for something that they desire and it doesn't manifest they can't understand the reason why it's not done.

In cases where this occurs, some Christians fall back on the theory that the promises of Jesus could not actually be literal. The Scripture is therefore downgraded by being interpreted through one's own personal experience of failure. This mentality can eventually lead one to embrace the old fallacy, "Jesus only meant that to be spiritual, not literal." This position is often reached by a Christian "trying" to believe what Jesus said but never meeting the conditions that joyfully qualify the promise.

Failure to receive can often be linked to doubts that overwhelm our faith. Doubts are fueled by the atmosphere of fear that permeates the natural realm in which we live. To receive from God, you must overpower unbelief with faith that stems from abiding in the Word of God. You must bring your faith to a point of *saturation*. One of my brothers-in-law went on a cruise not too long ago. Most cruise ships offer lavish buffet meals. He paid a premium price for him and his wife to make the journey, so he was intent on getting his money's worth out of the trip, and that included stuffing himself beyond normal capacity at every meal. At the conclusion of the seven-day voyage he had gained fourteen pounds. It was safe to say he was saturated with steak, lobster, and crab legs.

Just as you can be saturated with food and reach a point where you feel you can't eat one more bite, so must you do with your faith. Some believers endeavor to present themselves as being deeply spiritual and full of the Word of God, but in reality they are full of the evening news and submerged in sports, all governed by the television's remote control held firmly in their hand, which is wielded with an authority similar to the staff of Moses. Yet instead of splitting the Red Sea, they drown in doubt and find themselves unable to truly believe the promises of God.

Each day we are given 24 hours to use at our discretion. If a believer were to tithe two hours and forty minutes a day to the Lord, then his inner man, his spirit, would eventually reach a point of being saturated with the strong meat of God's Word, as well as with His presence and the glory of God. A good teaching CD, a YouTube video, or other format of hearing a faith-building message can easily cover an hour and a half, most of which could be done when driving a daily commute to work and back.

Getting up early to pray is very important, if not the most important spiritual discipline you could ever engage in. Kelly and I have two dogs. One of our smaller dogs, named Truffles, loves to spin in circles and chase her tail. Over the years we have watched Truffles continually try to catch up with her tail, but she has still never caught it. This is what it's like for the Christian who doesn't pray early in the morning—you'll be playing catch-up for the rest of the day, but you'll never capture the blessing and spiritual empowerment of that lost prayer time.

Over the years I have discovered that praying early in the morning when it is still dark outside seems to have a quantum leap effect on accessing spiritual power and heavenly insight. This type of prayer is very rich because it is coupled with the deep sacrifice of getting out of bed and meeting with the Lord at an offset time. This time frame allows for a greater increase of uninterrupted quietness which when taken advantage of will produce razor sharp focus in prayer. During these night sessions you will likely encounter the sensation that you have prayed for only a short amount of time, but upon checking a clock you discover that you have prayed much, much longer. This is the quantum effect that is produced through a combination of devotion, sacrifice, and acute focus. This may sound unorthodox and it's hard for me to describe it in words, but as you step into it you quickly discover there is a genuine realm of quantum glory where you are subtly clothed with the velvety blanketing of God's abiding presence. All of this unfolds while much of the world sleeps, as you sit there in the dark with the Lord in prayer and fellowship. You may find that midnight works well for you to pray, for others it may be sometime deeper into the night, or perhaps a while before sunrise. As you consistently attend your set time of prayer in the night, you will soon realize that this is a key component in manifesting the blessings of God.

After waking up and praying in the middle of the night, I will then go back to sleep for a few hours to get the required sleep my body needs in order to stay healthy. But just so you know, when it's time to wake up, if you lay in bed too long beyond your normal sleep requirements you will discover that the anointing you accumulated during your middle of the night prayer time will evaporate or be greatly diminished. It's similar to the manna that the children of Israel gathered while in the wilderness. Each morning they gathered manna, and when the sun became hot the manna that wasn't collected melted away. Just as the manna could evaporate, so too can the prayer anointing leave when a person chooses to lay around in bed longer than needed.

Oversleeping will also allow the archers to shoot at you. The archers are evil spirits that bombard your mind with thoughts or dreams that are impure, fear based, and troubling. If you just lethargically lie in bed longer than is required, then you are an easy target for them to hit. So, get up and be productive in life. John Wesley, the founder of the Methodist denomination, was an adamant believer that too much sleep was the cause of many sicknesses and illnesses, including many nervous disorders and eye problems.[1] He advocated that the normal person needs between six and eight hours of sleep nightly.

In 1995, I was in a meeting in Southern California in which the well-known evangelist Dr. Lester Sumrall was speaking. As he shared the great need to spread the gospel around the world, he paused in the middle of his sermon and said, "I hate beds." His reason for this statement was connected to a personal urgency in which he wanted to do all he could for the Lord while he still had the available time. He went home to be with the Lord the following year, having left behind a prodigious ministry that decades later is still reaching the lost.

Something I would like for you to consider is that if you oversleep one hour each day, you will therefore have overslept seven hours in one week. This means you have now overslept for 28 hours in a month and eventually will exceed 300 hours per year of squandering one of your most valuable resources—time. What productive work could you have done with those 300 hours if you were awake?

Three hundred hours is enough study time to easily pass the test to acquire a private pilot's license or earn a Class A commercial driver's license. Or you could use the time to become certified in a new trade or skill in order to earn a higher income. A strong walk with God does not come easy. It requires much personal discipline and a structured life that avoids lost and wasted time. This doesn't mean we overtax our bodies and never enjoy a Sabbath rest. I always take one day out of the week off to fully rest. On my Sabbath day of rest (usually Monday), the thought of work is not on my mind. It's a day to spend time with family and simply take it easy and enjoy God and His blessings. It's a time for my body to recuperate, my mind to meditate on something that's not work related, and to go slow throughout the day. I don't check e-mails, nor do I go to the office. It's a day that God endorses us to come to a standstill. Being in Jerusalem on the Sabbath day (Friday sundown to Saturday sundown) is always so refreshing because most of the city comes to a stop for twenty-four hours. Restaurants are closed, stores are not open, streets are quiet as the majority of residents honor this special day of rest. We must not underwork and be idle with our talents, but we also should seek to find the healthy balance of productivity and well-deserved rest. To abide in Christ and find time to meditate on His Word often involves the reshuffling of our priorities. Eventually there is a flow that is established of daily communion that we can peacefully maintain.

When you truly begin to abide in Christ, you will receive the desires you ask for. In this condition of abiding in Christ, you can discover that He will even give things to you that you have never formally asked for. Perhaps it was only a passing thought, something not even formed into a request that is expressed verbally in prayer, but yet it is manifested even before it was technically asked for through articulate speech.

Abiding in Christ also tapers the desire to ask God for things that are out of bounds due to the specific will of God pertaining to your life. There are some things I don't ask for because if I got them I know they would only serve to distract me from my calling and purpose. Oh yes, you will be blessed with wonderful blessings, but never forget you will have all eternity to do things in heaven that you may not have time to participate in while down here. Countless times I have been asked by ministers and relatives to go and play golf with them. But I don't play golf. People ask me, "Why don't you play golf?" My answer is simply, "Because I know I would like it." I already have a full plate; I don't want to put something else on there that isn't necessary and may even hinder my devotional time with the Lord.

Jesus said, "If you abide in Me." The word *if* is conditional. If the conditions are met, then the promise is accessed. If the conditions are not met, then we must trim out interruptions, distractions, unnecessary weights, and any hindrance that impedes our spiritual progress. It is a personal choice we all make every day we live. Press in today to a place of continual abiding in Christ. Saturate your thinking with His words. Then Jesus will be sure to fulfill His promise to you of manifesting your requested desires.

NOTE

1. John Wesley, "Sermon 93: On Redeeming the Time," Global Ministries, accessed September 8, 2016, http://www .umcmission.org/Find-Resources/John-Wesley-Sermons/ Sermon-93-On-Redeeming-The-Time.

Chapter Three

SHOW ME YOUR WORKS

Throughout the Bible we see countless stories of miracles received by those who used their faith. When you examine their stories even closer, you begin to see that every person who received from God had faith with corresponding works. Adding works to your faith is the necessary validity that says you are serious about what you believe. It is also evidence that you are expecting to receive. Your faith will never take flight if it doesn't have works to go along with it. The second chapter of the book of James is one of the best resources for understanding the inseparable need to combine faith and works. Let's examine a few of the highlights that are mentioned by James.

> *What does it profit, my brethren, if someone says he has faith but does not have works? Can faith save him?* (James 2:14)

There are various Christians who have a form of faith, but their faith is incomplete due to the absence of works. James asks, "Can faith save him?" In other words, he's asking if this type of incomplete faith can get the job done. The answer, of course, is no. As we examine this subject of faith and corresponding works, I would like you to consider your personal faith projects and what specific works you are doing to show your faith. We should all have faith projects that we are working on. Your faith likes projects, and if you don't supply it with a good assignment, you will stagnate spiritually.

> *If a brother or sister is naked and destitute of daily food, and one of you says to them, "Depart in peace, be warmed and filled," but you do not give them the things which are needed for the body, what does it profit? Thus also faith by itself, if it does not have works, is dead* (James 2:15–17).

One of the reasons for the avoidance of attaching works to faith is because it offers an escape from personal responsibility. It's easy to say, "Depart in peace, be warmed and filled," because that requires very little effort on our part. We may pray and ask for God to use us for His glory by helping a poor family that He places in our path, but then if we skip the corresponding works when we have an opportunity to act our faith remains dead and we do not profit anyone. We certainly cannot help everyone, but we can help those whom God assigns to us through His divine plan. The Christian who does not have works connected to his faith is the person who will still be in the same place of spiritual bareness five, ten, and twenty years from now. We must do more than pray and fast. We must do more than hear good teaching. We must move forward in faith by identifying certain works that we can perform regarding our specific faith project.

> *Show me your faith without your works, and I will show you my faith by my works* (James 2:18b).

James said he would show you his faith by his works. How can you see faith when it is described by many as an intangible substance? Faith is revealed through outward actions that give verification of what you believe. In this world you will discover there are many arm-chair critics who are envious of those who have broken through into the realms of God's blessings. These are the ones (including some

Christians) who sit back and pass judgment and critique the works of others while they never leave their own seats of comfort to accomplish anything noble or significant. They have learned Christian clichés and religious lingo to appear spiritually qualified, but in the end they are still stuck on the perpetual plateau of dead faith because they do not have corresponding works.

> *You believe that there is one God. You do well. Even the demons believe—and tremble!* (James 2:19)

James did not suddenly switch to a new subject and begin a discourse on demonology. The context is still the same, but he is now using another example to prove that faith without works is dead. A Christian is a person who has heard the preaching of the gospel and responded to it by receiving Jesus as Savior and Lord. In other words, we did more than just listen to the gospel—we responded to it. A response shows works being tied to our faith. The demons also believe in God. They know that God is real to the point that they tremble when they think about it or hear the name of Jesus mentioned. But don't ever expect a demon to do anything further with their belief in God. No demon is ever going to attach a good work to their belief in God, despite the fact that they know that God exists.

This is why demons have dead faith—because they have no intention of ever changing. Their future is sealed and they are headed to the lake of fire to suffer in flaming torment for all eternity. A few years ago a very misguided Christian approached me and asked me to pray for the devil so that the devil might repent and be saved. But this is a prayer that can never be answered because it is contrary to the Bible, which states that the lake of fire was prepared for the devil and his angels (see Matt. 25:41) and that Satan will be cast into the lake of fire and brimstone along with the beast and the false prophet, and they will be tormented day and night forever and ever (see Rev. 20:10).

Demons believe in God but have no works. Let us distance ourselves from dead faith and this deceptive way of thinking by adding works to our faith.

> *But do you want to know, O foolish man, that faith without works is dead? Was not Abraham our father justified by works when he offered Isaac his son on the altar?* (James 2:20-21)

Here we see James identify the person who does not apply works to his faith as being a "foolish" man. Anyone who disagrees with any portion of the truth of God's Word is acting foolishly. Truth never changes. Truth is eternal and its principles remain the same regardless of how many new generations come forth upon the earth. It's when we try to redefine the truth that we get into trouble. No matter how much a person may disagree with this particular truth of biblical faith, it remains unchanged that faith without works is dead.

We have heard countless stories about the great faith of Abraham. But James is very wise to bring out the full expression of Abraham's faith that was displayed through his works. Consider all of the works that went into Abraham's effort to sacrifice his son Isaac upon the altar. His first work was simply to obey the command of God and make preparations to do what God instructed him to do—offer his son as a sacrifice. Second, he arose early the next morning to start on his journey. The work and effort of getting up early, packing food, saddling the donkey, informing two of his young workers to quickly get ready and come along, splitting the wood for the burnt offering, and then riding a donkey and walking for three days to Mount Moriah were valid works that expressed his belief. No amount of prayer and fasting will ever substitute for obedience. When God has told you to do something you don't need to pray about it; you just need to go do it.

The intensity of Abraham's works escalated upon reaching the summit of Mount Moriah. Bold works were displayed as Abraham built an altar and laid the wood in order. He then bound Isaac, his son, and laid him on the altar, upon the wood. Then Abraham stretched out his hand and took the knife to slay his son. Here is where we see the words of James ringing forth with a startling clarity, "Was not Abraham our father justified by works...?" (James 2:21). You will never pass the test of faith until you demonstrate corresponding works. If we desire to replicate the success of Abraham, then we need to follow Abraham's pattern and thus incorporate works into our faith projects.

> *Do you see that faith was working together with his works,*
> *and by works faith was made perfect?* (James 2:22)

Perfect faith can only be reached through spiritual growth and maturity. It requires us to accept our own personal responsibilities and not rely upon others to do what is our obligation. Spiritual growth is parallel to natural growth. A baby needs lots of help. He has to be fed and have his diaper changed. Eventually he grows out of this stage and can begin to learn to do the basics by himself. Wouldn't it be strange to see a full-grown man in his thirties wearing a diaper? All joking aside, we would all think, "Something has gone acutely wrong here; that man has not mentally developed properly." Our heavenly Father expects for us to grow up spiritually just as we do naturally. When you are a young Christian and newly saved you can ride the spiritual coattails of someone else. Others may pray for you and their faith may carry you, but eventually you are going to have to start using your own faith. This is like the baby eagle being nudged out of the nest so that he can learn to use his wings and fly and not depend on his mother to bring his food to him, but rather mature and gather his own food and other necessities of life.

Perfect faith is a place where you have mastered the art of combining faith with the appropriate works. Once this level is achieved, you transition to a new level in your relationship with God. This new level is called "friendship" with God.

> And he [Abraham] was called the friend of God (James 2:23b).

When you understand the principles of faith, you begin to understand God because you see how He operates. He is a faith God. Faith is what is required to please Him. Unbelief is what displeases Him. Unbelief not only disqualifies us from the blessings of God but it also distorts the way we perceive Him. When we believe God and add works to our faith, we then merge into a walk with God of mutual understanding. Friendship is often based around a mutual interest or the love of a shared belief. God loves mature faith. The more you exercise mature faith by demonstrating your works, the more you and your Father have in common, which leads to a deeper friendship. In other words, you get a lot more out of this than the manifestation of a miracle or whatever it might be that you are trusting God to do. Yes, you get your miracle, but you also come into friendship with God—a highly favorable position, indeed.

When Kelly and I were first married, I had a desire to purchase a new motorcycle. I had owned several before and sold them over time, so I thought it would be nice to acquire a new one. While meditating on the teachings of James about combining faith and works, I realized I needed to identify a specific work that I could combine with my faith for a motorcycle. I decided I would make my work assignment locating a dedicated place to park my motorcycle once it arrived. This may sound like it was an easy task, but it wasn't because our business was located in a highly trafficked shopping center that had no "dedicated" parking spots, even for store owners. After thinking the situation over,

I decided the best place to park my new motorcycle would be right in front of my business, up on the extra wide sidewalk, in front of my main store window. I actually marked the area off with colored tape, and every day when I went to work I would look at that spot and say, "That's where I'm going to park my new motorcycle." It was only about two months later when Kelly and I received an unexpected financial blessing that allowed us to go down to the motorcycle dealership and pay cash for the bike of our choice, a Suzuki RF 600R sport bike. It was a wonderful experience to drive that beautiful bike to my office and park it in the very spot that I had prepared for it. The moment felt somewhat surreal, almost like a feeling of "that was too easy." When faith and works are joined together it's like putting your hand into a perfect fitting glove—they both complement each other and blend together seamlessly.

Many years ago I ministered in a certain church that I had spoken in previously. It had been about a year since I last ministered in this particular church, and when I spoke there again many of the same people were in attendance. After completing my time of ministry, the pastor asked me if I could meet him in his private office to discuss a matter that had arisen with one of his female church members. In my spirit I immediately sensed that something was not right and that the pastor was not being forthcoming about his intent.

Joining us in his office was the church member he had mentioned—a woman who appeared to be in her early thirties. Accompanying her and the pastor was one of the church elders. Once we were all seated the pastor said, "Steven, this woman said that last year when you came here and ministered you prophesied over her in the service that she would be married within one year. She is still single and is saddened about her present situation of still being unmarried." I informed the pastor that I never gave a prophecy stating she would be married within a year. I explained that I did encourage her to use her faith for a spouse and that she should trust the Lord for a godly mate. I also reminded the pastor that all personal ministry and every personal prophecy I gave to his members was with his elders standing next to me and took place in the public assembly.

The elder who was present had a tape player and said, "I just located the audio tape from Steven's visit here last year. Let's replay the tape and listen to what he actually said." Upon playing the tape I was immediately vindicated (thank God for evidence). The words I spoke to the single woman were basically words of encouragement and did not include any type of a one-year prophetic promise. In her mind she had added to what I said and then wrongly insinuated that I gave an errant prophecy. The way in which the pastor handled the situation was inappropriate because he had already chosen to side with her rather than be slow to hear and slow to judge. He should have located and listened to the audio tape *before* even calling a meeting.

Nevertheless, I could still see the sadness in the heart of the woman who wanted so strongly to get married. Having compassion, I offered to pray for her, which she accepted. After I prayed there seemed to hang in the air a type of animosity that flowed from this woman and the pastor toward me. The Holy Spirit showed me that both her and the pastor blamed God for not bringing a godly spouse into her life. This woman was like a spiritual daughter to the pastor, so together they seemed to form a sort of mutual consolation in finding fault against God for their unanswered prayer. Their disappointment in God was reflected in a diminished view of me as a minister that was not expressed directly in words but rather in a distasteful attitude that was palpable.

Having completed my meetings there I focused my attention to my busy schedule of travel. About three weeks later I was in a different state ministering for several days. While there I had a remarkable visitation from the Lord Jesus in the hotel room in which

I was staying. Appearing to me in a vision that I wasn't expecting, the Lord came and shared several things about my ministry that were encouraging and helpful. These things He shared were normal insights that you might find on the regular menu of ministry work. But then He brought up something that was not on my ministry list of things to do. Standing before me, I heard and saw Him just as clearly as seeing a person in physical form, although I was having a vision. What I am going to share is word for word what Jesus told me. I would be lying if I said that Jesus did not appear to me and say this, but He did. Jesus is the most honest person you will ever meet. He can be so blunt and to the point, not mincing words, and He tells the truth even if it's not what you are expecting to hear or wanting to hear. So I would like to share with you what the Lord told me.

He said, "I want to talk with you about the woman who has been unable to get married. She says she wants to get married. She says she has faith for a husband. But if she wants to get married, then why does she dress and present herself like a nun who wants to join a convent?" (I told you He was honest.) Instantly, I saw what He was referring to. In the recent and previous time when I saw this woman while ministering at her home church, she always looked disheveled. She wore old, faded-out blue jeans, her hair was never styled, and she never wore makeup. She was never neat or sharp in her appearance and not once wore anything new or nice. Her unkempt level of dressing actually made her appear much older, like that of an old maid. Then the Lord said, "She says she has faith to get married, but how come she never wears beautiful perfume?" As He spoke these words to me, it was obvious that the Lord's displeasure about her false accusations against Him did not sit well with Him. He was not smiling when He spoke these words, but was rather stern against her excuses to assign blame to others.

Let us always remember that the Lord wants to help. He will do everything in His power to help, but He will not do our part for us.

In no uncertain terms the Lord conveyed to me that it was her lack of producing any identifiable work that kept her single. It wasn't God's fault or my fault. After saying this, the Lord left and the vision ended. The Lord conveyed it very clearly to me that this woman had faith without corresponding works; therefore, her faith for a husband was dead and unproductive. This vision also supernaturally lifted any trace of blame or false responsibility off of me that the pastor had tried to put on me through his misconstrued reasoning.

I guess someone may be wondering, "Pastor Steven, after the vision, did you get on the phone and call the pastor and tell him and that woman why she doesn't have a husband?" No, I never told them a word even though I ran into this woman in Jerusalem (of all places) a few years later. She was still single and had traveled to Israel by herself to visit the Holy Land. I had just finished praying for the sick in a miracle healing service at the Steps of Ascension at the southern edge of the Temple Mount. She was casually walking around Jerusalem when to her amazement she saw me ministering to a group of about four hundred people. She waited for me to finish ministering in order to politely greet Kelly and me.

There are probably some who will think, "Did you tell her what she needed to do in order to get married?" No, I didn't tell her because she didn't ask. The vision that took place several years earlier was for my sake in order to remove any false sense of burden that her pastor had tried to place upon me. If she had asked for insight concerning her marital barrenness, I would have been happy to have shared with her that she needed to add works to her faith, but she didn't ask. Always remember, the Lord Jesus is a gentleman. If you don't ask Him, there are some things He won't bring up, even if you desperately want to know. He said in His Word, "Ask, and it will be given to you," and, "For everyone who asks receives" (Matt. 7:7-8). Just wanting to know is not enough. We must be humble and ask the Lord for insight into any area of unfruitfulness. Asking represents humility. Asking conveys the truth that someone else may have deeper insight into a situation than we do. The grace to receive answers is supplied to those who are humble enough to ask. I do truly hope that the dear Christian sister in the Lord caught the revelation of faith *and* works. If she did, then I have no doubt she has a wedding ring on her finger at this time.

Today, I want you to identify a specific work that you can attach to your faith project. As you progress toward the manifestation of what you are believing for, be aware that you may need to add a few more works along the way. But whatever stage you are in, you can start right now. Oftentimes it is not so much that we are waiting for the Lord to act as it is that He's waiting for us to act though our works. Ask the Lord to help you pinpoint a work that reflects what it is you are believing God to do. The Holy Spirit will help bring forth this thought of a corresponding work into your mind. Even if the specific work seems small, it is at least the beginning of evidence that God needs to put your faith project in the official book of heaven's "valid project" list. The Holy Spirit will lead you each step of the way till you cross the finish line of "there it is, manifested in my life." Until then, keep up the good work.

Chapter Four

THE MIND TRANSFORMATION PROCESS

Your mind is the most valuable asset you have on this earth. With a renewed mind you can safely navigate through the choppy waters of life and into the calm harbor of the blessings of God. It is up to you to take care of your mind and ensure that it is transformed through the word of God. Scientists have now discovered that every time you think a thought it creates a small line upon your brain. The initial line is so small that it cannot be seen with the human eye. But whenever you rethink the same thought that same neurological pathway in your brain is traveled on again, and the line becomes more established. If you think the same thought hundreds or thousands of times, then the line has now developed into a deep groove that supports a fixed way of thinking. When wrong thoughts have been established, we must retrain our brains and establish new pathways that are in agreement with the Word of God. This is not easy to do because it involves rewiring our brains, but it is possible and the results that are yielded make it very worthwhile.

> *And do not be conformed to this world, but be transformed*
> *by the renewing of your mind, that you may prove what is*

that good and acceptable and perfect will of God (Romans 12:2).

When I was young I remember the local railroad that ran nearby our house out in the country. Oftentimes when we were traveling somewhere by car we would have to stop and wait at the railroad tracks while the passing train went by. My dad would turn off the car engine and sometimes we would get out of the car to get a better view of the train as it went by. Normally it would take about seven minutes for the full train to pass. I enjoyed every minute of watching it.

As time passed eventually we moved out of the area and to a different state. About thirty years later I went back to the same area for a family reunion. To my surprise many things had not changed. Poverty was still high in the area. The former dirt/gravel county road that we once drove on had now been paved with asphalt, which was a nice upgrade. I could still recognize many local landmarks and physical features of the land. There was one thing, however, that threw off my ability to fully orientate my whereabouts. I couldn't find the train track anywhere. I asked my dad about it and he told me that years back the railroad deemed that particular freight route to be no longer profitable, so they discontinued the route and completely removed the tracks, including the rails and crossties. I then drove to where the railroad track used to be and noticed that where a major rail line used to operate was now nothing but fully grown forest. It was as if the railroad tracks had never been there before.

The neurological pathways in your brain function similar to a railroad track. The renewing of the mind involves the laying down of a new track. It also requires the absolute dismantling of former rail lines that transported the former unproductive freight of fear, worry, poverty thinking, sickness mentality, greed, lust, and all other forms of corrupt cargo. When the old rail lines of sinful thought are removed, then your brain can find its proper, God-given place of chemical balance. The transformation process of your mind is a multistage process, and one process you need to be aware of is the *detox stage* or what may be better described simply as *withdrawal symptoms*.

Particularly in the southern states of America there are thousands upon thousands of Christians who are saved, love Jesus, and who smoke cigarettes daily. Even though they know that smoking is directly linked to cancer they still smoke, even before and after church services. I know this personally because I live in North Carolina (one of the world's leading exporters of tobacco), and I've ministered in many churches where it's very difficult for some members to sit through an hour-long service. As soon as the service is over there are those who rush out in order to light up a stogie to get that quick nicotine fix. The renewing of the mind is more than just discovering the will of God, which is expressed in the Bible. It is also the laborious process of change and transformation from something that is a negative to that which is a plus. There can be times when God immediately delivers His people and certain impure desires are immediately vaporized and gone by the power of the Holy Spirit. But most of the time God requires us to go through the normal transformation process of step-by-step renewing our minds and experiencing the painful withdrawal symptoms so that we have no desire to turn back to Egypt.

Anyone who has overcome the addiction to tobacco products will tell you that you will have a real battle on your hands if you choose to abandon the practice. Can it be done? Absolutely. Is it easy? No, it's extremely difficult because your mind has been trained to become accustomed to the usage of tobacco and the release of over 4,000 toxic and addictive substances such as nicotine, tar, carbon monoxide, ammonia, arsenic, and other carcinogens that are released as you inhale the smoke. It's as if a railroad line has been put in place within the person's brain and they keep traveling that path even though they know it will eventually lead to a somber trip to the hospital with a grievous diagnosis.

Unhealthy eating habits have influenced the lives of many Christians in North America in a way that has led to heart disease, stroke, high blood pressure, diabetes, sleep apnea, breathing problems, and some forms of cancer. This is rooted in a brain problem and requires the biblical principle of renewing the mind in order to transition into God's plan of divine health. The indulgence of fried and sugary foods is known to release surges of the hormone dopamine in your brain. Dopamine is often referred to as the "happy hormone" because it helps control the brain's reward and pleasure center. When you indulge in junk food and processed snacks and eat things that are highly saturated in fat, dopamine levels spike, causing you to crave more and more. The next thing you know you've eaten the whole bag of potato chips or downed the entire tub of ice cream.

The biblical process of renewing the mind requires us to take up tracks where the former railroad ran and let our brains return to a normal and balanced state. Getting back to normal will take us through a detox stage in which we experience unpleasant withdrawal symptoms. Your brain becomes accustomed to certain foods that trigger the release of dopamine. When you stop eating those harmful foods, your brain will soon throw a fit because it has gotten chemically dependent upon them. Renewing the mind is not easy because we face withdrawal symptoms with almost everything that is harmful to us that we wish to quit. The good part is that withdrawal symptoms during the renewing process are at their most unpleasant state for the first two weeks. After that it will get much easier.

In the 1930s, scientists thought that the only two types of addiction were alcohol and drugs, such as cocaine or heroin. Only in the last generation have scientists begun to understand that our brains can be altered through many different stimulants. With the advent of the Internet there has been an unprecedented wave of men and women becoming addicted to Internet pornography. Many of God's people have been trapped in bondage through this snare of the enemy. Some experts in the field of neurology have said that overcoming the addiction to Internet pornography can be more difficult and the withdrawal symptoms more severe than that of a person who is coming off an addiction to heroin. The reason for this is that viewing Internet porn releases massive amounts of dopamine into a person's brain, far beyond what would normally be released. This enormous amount of dopamine that is released is essentially like the brain building a mega railroad track that is deeply entrenched and heavily traveled upon for hours each day over a period of months and years. Our brains are designed to establish reward pathways. When we do something that provides a reward, our brains record the experience and we are likely to do it again. In the real world, rewards usually only come with effort and are achieved over a span of time. Certain drugs and stimulants—whether it's marijuana, Internet porn, cigarettes, alcohol, endless shopping, masturbation, gambling, or eating the whole box of Twinkies—provide the brain a shortcut to experience the reward sensation by flooding the brain with dopamine.

To reverse this process with the biblical method of renewing the mind will initially be very difficult and will be associated with extreme withdrawal symptoms such as depression, nausea, vomiting, inability to focus or concentrate, chills, fever, loss of appetite, nervousness, panic attacks, and many other symptoms that anyone with an addiction of any kind experiences during a detox. You must be willing to allow the process of renewing the mind to work its way through the various stages, especially that of the withdrawal stage. If you quit and go back to the former practice, you will lose the precious ground you have gained and you will have to start over from the beginning and make another attempt. As the gifted writer and humorist Mark Twain once said of his tobacco habit, "Giving up smoking is the easiest thing in the world. I know because I've done it thousands of times."

Even ministers aren't exempt from having to renew their minds. It can be just as much a struggle for them as it can be for anyone else. Consider the time when the world-famous evangelist Dwight L. Moody went to London to meet Charles Spurgeon, who at that time had the largest church in the world. The story goes that when Moody went to see Spurgeon, Spurgeon answered the door with a cigar in his mouth. Upon seeing this, Moody almost fell down the stairs in shock. Moody asked Spurgeon how he, a great man of God, could be a smoker. Spurgeon walked over to Moody and, placing his finger on Moody's obese stomach, said, "The same way you, a man of God, could be that fat!" Moody weighed almost 300 pounds and passed away at the early age of 62. Spurgeon eventually gave up smoking due to his ill health and his realization that it was not a good influence for young people. He died at the age of only 57.

Throughout his ministry, Moody preached to huge crowds that totaled over 10,000,000 people in his lifetime. Spurgeon was known as the Prince of Preachers and his brilliant messages are still read by thousands today. But ministers aren't exempt from having to obey Romans, the twelfth chapter and the second verse. Whether it's smoking, overeating, nervous disorders, unclean habits, or a host of other problems from the menagerie of trouble that besets the human race, it is clear to see that we all have things we need to work on and it takes effort. We each face an individual responsibility to renew our minds with the Word of God and be committed to the process of being transformed fully into the image of Christ. I can't renew your mind for you. If you don't take care of your mind, then nobody else will. If we do not renew our minds, we will stay bound to certain behavioral patterns that keep us from accessing the blessings of God.

This Book of the Law shall not depart from your mouth, but you shall meditate in it day and night, that you may observe to do according to all that is written in it. For then you will make your way prosperous, and then you will have good success (Joshua 1:8).

Renewing our minds will consist heavily of meditating upon how God's Word instructs us to live. Wrong ways of thinking, talking, and acting can be transformed when we replace such actions with the light of God's Word. How do you remove darkness from a room? You do so by turning on the light. This is known as the law of displacement. In other words, we not only stop wrong methods of thinking, but we replace them with something else to fill the empty void. We are to fill our lives with the Word of God and live by its principles and then we will experience prosperity and good success.

When Paul told us to renew our mind he was referring to an ongoing work. The word for "renew" in the New Testament Greek language meant "to renovate and make brand new." Kelly and I love to watch shows that feature old homes being renovated into new condition. Often this involves seeing a home stripped of its old and fire-prone electrical wiring and upgraded with a modern system that is safe and energy efficient. Our favorite part, however, is what takes place with the master bath and the kitchen. By gutting these rooms of their outdated and worn condition they can be made brand new by then installing marble floors, granite countertops, beautiful wood cabinets, and new fixtures. Gone is the former look of the 1970s that has now been transformed into something anyone would desire to live in. With new plumbing, a new HVAC system, and better insulation the home becomes more functional and more comfortable. This type of *renovation* is exactly what the Scripture refers to when it speaks of renewing your mind. It means to renovate old, dilapidated mind-sets with safe and stable biblical mind-sets that position you for comfort and enduring success. This metamorphosis doesn't unfold overnight, but like a home remodel your hard work will soon be visible to yourself and others.

Scientists today have a technical expression for what the Bible revealed to us thousands of years ago. Scientists call this process of renewing the mind *neuroplasticity*. In laymen's terms, this means that your brain has the ability to change. *Neuro* refers to your brain, and *plasticity* speaks of the ability to change from a present condition into something entirely different. The brain has a remarkable ability to adapt by creating new neural pathways. You really can teach an old brain new tricks. Your brain has the ability to create new brain cells and to learn indefinitely. There is virtually no limit to what you can learn. You can use certain parts of your brain and develop them more highly then other people who don't use them. An example is seen in London taxi drivers who use the part of the brain known as the hippocampus more than London bus drivers, causing it to grow larger. Why would this be? Because by driving the same route every day the bus driver isn't required to exercise his brain as much. However, the cab driver depends on it constantly to help him get through the myriad of streets in London.

We can restrict our brains by embracing a poverty mentality. Or we can renew our minds with what God said concerning finances and step into His ability to empower us to a place of financial dominion and overflow. Poverty thinking can be a real challenge to reverse. I know because I went through this and am still working every day to renew my mind to what God said as compared to what misguided religious tradition taught me when I was being raised. My family grew up thinking it was God's will for us to be poor and financially broke. The preacher said we weren't supposed to have any of this old world's goods. He said it, we foolishly believed it, and we suffered in lack and want. The financial covenant that was available for us to walk in was something completely veiled to us. We all have areas in our thinking that need to be renovated, remodeled, and made new. Nobody on planet earth is exempt from this required task. To neglect your mind is to neglect your marvelous inheritance that you are called to possess.

Perhaps you have allowed your mind to travel down the wrong track for too long. Change is possible through the goodness and kindness of God. The gospel of Jesus Christ is a seed that can be planted in your mind, which then matures and is able to remove every weed of wrong thinking. What commitment do we need to make to ensure that this growth remains permanent? The following verses give us a guideline that will produce positive lasting results.

> *Therefore you shall lay up these words of mine in your heart and in your soul, and bind them as a sign on your hand, and they shall be as frontlets between your eyes. You shall teach them to your children, speaking of them when you sit in your house, when you walk by the way, when you lie down, and when you rise up. And you shall write them on the doorposts of your house and on your gates* (Deuteronomy 11:18–20).

If you've spent decades functioning in a poverty mindset, you are not going to establish new neurological pathways of prosperity within your brain by only listening to one sermon. You will need to listen to hundreds of sermons. You must keep the truth of biblical prosperity before you day and night; when you go to sleep and when you wake up it must be on your mind. This is the only way in which a prosperity mind-set can be developed.

If you have struggled with being overweight and in related poor health, then you must determine to stop letting the food industry manipulate your brain. Healthy weight loss and a physically fit body begin in the brain. Learn to recognize how worldly marketing techniques are used against your mind to influence you to eat foods that can easily cause you to pile on the pounds. You'll never see an ad on television for prunes that guarantees happiness. But an ice cream commercial can be made to appear heavenly. The name of the flavor will not just be "chocolate ice cream" but rather "ultra-rich cookie dough double overload chocolate ice cream." When food is associated with a pleasurable experience and viewed over and over by the mind, then eventually you will want to experience this sensation. The marketing world also knows that certain colors inspire various feelings. Red will energize you. Blue will calm you. Yellow makes you feel happy. If the dye and artificial food coloring were removed from your favorite drink, would you still drink it if it were grey? God designed your brain with a reward system that is made to engage in behavior that brings pleasure, such as eating tasty food. When we eat junk food the reward circuits within our brain are activated and the chemical dopamine is released. Fatty, greasy, sugary, and salt-laden foods can overwhelm our brains with pleasure and distort our reward system. The brain responds by adapting and making more receptors for dopamine. Eventually, a greater amount of junk food is needed to get the same "high," making us eat more in the same way that an addict develops a tolerance for drugs. We know junk food is bad for our bodies, but we continue to eat it. It's very tasty, it's all around us, it doesn't cost much, and it's hard to resist. It affects our bodies with unwanted extra weight; it is proven to cause inflammation in the brain and shrinks the brain's learning capabilities. How can a Christian be free from something that is so enticing? Freedom comes through the renewing (renovating) of the mind and knowing that the grace and compassion of God will carry us through the transformation process.

> *For we do not have a High Priest who cannot sympathize*
> *with our weaknesses, but was in all points tempted as we*
> *are, yet without sin (Hebrews 4:15).*

Jesus can sympathize with our weaknesses. He had more than just a knowledge of our condition; He actually experienced our condition. He was tempted, He was persecuted, He was despised, He suffered physical pain, He endured mental agony, He died the most sorrowful of all deaths—all of this without succumbing to sin. He knows how difficult it can be for us to let go of something that we enjoy but that is also counterproductive to our life and His will. Expect His grace to be upon you as you journey through the various stages of renewing your mind with the word of God. The outcome will be truly glorious because it opens the gateway to all of the blessings that God has made available to you.

Chapter Five

LEARNING FAITH FROM THE NIGHTHAWK

Faith to do the impossible can be directly linked to hearing the voice of God and receiving the *rhema* word. To be successful in your faith endeavors it is essential that you can hear from God, who is alive and still speaks today. I want to direct your understanding to the revelation that those believers who have a deep spiritual walk with God and can discern the leading voice of the Holy Spirit are the ones who have the potential to pull off great exploits of faith. Faith is a spiritual component. It functions best within those who are spiritual. Jesus stood at the apex of being spiritual. His devotional life with the heavenly Father was paramount and came before all ministry needs and demands. The earthshaking ministry of Jesus was a by-product of His rich devotional life. Faith thrives in spirituality. Faith withers when your prayer time weakens. Faith and prayer are forever intertwined. If your prayer time goes downhill, then your faith will suffer immediately. You can quote the Scripture until your voice is harsh and your throat is sore, but it will not have inherent power unless it is supported through prayer.

Because of the eternal link that connects vibrant faith to spirituality (prayer and time spent with God), we need to dig deeper into the devotional life of Jesus and rediscover His devotional methods in order to achieve similar results in the realm of faith and the miraculous. We can begin this journey by examining an ancient bird of Israel identified in the Bible as the *nighthawk*. When we look at certain characteristics of this bird we see prophetic symbolism that carries profound meaning. I really believe Jesus was a nighthawk. No, I haven't gone cuckoo by believing Jesus was a bird. What I'm referring to is a person who is active at certain times of the night. Let's begin our study of this, and I pray that as you consider this teaching you find your wings and begin to fly not only during the day but at night as well.

> *Of all clean birds ye shall eat. But these are they of which ye shall not eat: the eagle, and the ossifrage, and the ospray, and the glede, and the kite, and the vulture after its kind, and every raven after his kind, and the owl, and the night hawk, and the cuckow, and the hawk after his kind* (Deuteronomy 14:11–15 KJV).

Israel is known as being one of the best places in the world to enjoy watching birds and their migration. When Kelly and I host tours to Israel we try to schedule a certain Israeli friend as our tour guide who possesses deep knowledge of the biblical and historic sites, along with the added benefit that he also happens to love wildlife, especially birds. His knowledge of the native animals of Israel always comes out as we tour the Holy Land. For instance, we can be driving along in our bus near the Jordan River while hearing him discuss the biblical site we are passing by. Suddenly he will interrupt his normal discourse and point toward the window with excitement, "There's a black heron just to your left, there by the water," or "Notice the beautiful kingfisher sitting on the pole nearby us." Israel is blessed by God in many ways. Their unique location allows the country to experience the best that nature can offer.

Twice a year over 500 million birds pass through Israel, making it one of the most impressive aerial superhighways on the planet. Israel is positioned as a land bridge between the three continents of Africa, Europe, and Asia. Dr. Yossi Lesham, the nation's leading bird expert, says, "Israel sits on the junction of three continents. Politically, it's a disaster, but for bird migration, it's heaven."

Complete populations containing hundreds of species migrate through Israel in the fall on their way to the wintering grounds in Africa and then back again in the spring. The Sea of Galilee with its lush habitat is a major refueling and resting place for many of these birds. This area is within the middle of what is called the Great Rift Valley, which stretches from northern Syria all the way to central Mozambique in Africa.

The valley creates warm thermal currents that the birds ride on from Africa to Europe. These thermals make flying much easier for the birds as compared to flying over the waters of the Mediterranean Sea. The narrow Great Rift Valley that extends through Israel creates a natural "bottleneck," which these birds find to be the most convenient route to travel. It's a wonder of nature to see so many different types of birds in such large numbers in a nation that is so small in land mass.

Today Israel has become a "birding mega center" that has birthed an entirely new recreational culture over the past few years. Both professional and amateur birders, photographers, and experts from all over the world come to see this natural wonder. Dr. Lesham explains that, "In one morning, we can see maybe 10,000 eagles. Just in one morning." There is an annual bird festival in the Hula Valley, just north of the Sea of Galilee. Each year the bird sanctuary there attracts over 400,000 visitors and 50,000 dedicated bird watchers. In light of this amazing phenomenon of birds it would be wise to consider the following prophecy concerning the last days that still must be fulfilled.

Then I saw an angel standing in the sun; and he cried with a loud voice, saying to all the birds that fly in the midst of heaven, "Come and gather together for the supper of the great God, that you may eat the flesh of kings, the flesh of captains, the flesh of mighty men, the flesh of horses and of those who sit on them, and the flesh of all people, free and slave, both small and great" (Revelation 19:17-18).

All of the evil forces that come against Israel in the battle of Armageddon will be destroyed by the Lord. Those who wish for the destruction of Israel and go into battle to destroy her will not succeed. The ungodly will be defeated and their dead bodies will be left in the open fields for the millions of birds to feast upon. We don't have to concern ourselves in the least bit if the angel can gather up enough birds for the supper of God. We know that there certainly isn't any lack of birds passing through Israel to fulfill their part in this specific Bible prophecy! Whenever you see news reports on television showing hate-filled mobs in the Middle East chanting in repetitive unison, "Death to Israel!" just be mindful that unless these people repent and turn to Christ then many will eventually be having an appointment with an army of over half a billion hungry birds at "the supper of God."

There are many fascinating and beautiful birds in Israel. The rose-ringed parakeet has gorgeous lime green and soft yellow colors. The strange but brilliant bird called the hoopoe defends itself by bending over and squirting fecal matter right into the eyes of its predator. It also bathes in its anal excretions to deter parasites and bacterial infections. This bird's determination, grit, and creative methods of defending itself are some of the key reasons it has been chosen to be the national bird of Israel. Like the hoopoe, you have to admire Israel's ingenuity to survive against all odds, as it is surrounded by twenty-two Islamic nations that long to see Israel destroyed through any available means. These nations that strive against Israel do not include the terrorist populations that have burgeoned out from these Islamic countries such as Hamas, Hezbollah, ISIS, Al-Qaeda, the Muslim Brotherhood, and many other lesser-known terrorist organizations that conduct jihad and ongoing work to implement Sharia law throughout the earth.

Fiery rhetoric and steady conflict are directed against Israel from Iran to Indonesia as well as throughout many Western nations. Various wars in the Middle East that are staged against Israel are inevitable, eventually leading to the granddaddy of all wars, which will be Armageddon. The Israelis are a very resilient people. One day they can be putting on gas masks preparing for war, and then later when things settle down they are back outside enjoying festivities, playing sports, going to concerts, and watching birds. We should always pray for the peace of Jerusalem and for the nation of Israel as a whole. We should pray that America come alongside Israel and be a strong shoulder of support to her. God raised up America to play a key role in the rebirth of Israel, and America has a prophetic destiny to be a defender of Israel.

I would like to point out a very special bird mentioned in the Bible that accomplishes much of its mission through stealth and covert operations. If you are a former military special ops person, then I believe you will connect with the roots of special ops missions, which is based primarily upon night raids. If you ever dreamed about being on a special forces unit, then now's your time to enlist and take your place in the spiritual night brigade. This unit is open to men and women, and there are even some children and teens who have secured a position within its ranks. The bird we want to examine in the Scripture is the mysterious nighthawk. The nighthawk is mentioned twice in the Bible. The Hebrew word for "nighthawk" is *tachmas,* which means to "tear or scratch the face." The word *tachmas* can also be translated as "the violent one." Noted scholar Adam Clarke, in his biblical commentary on the nighthawk, said that this bird was known not just to the Israelites, but to the Arabs in Egypt and also those living in Syria. Clarke quoted from the earlier explorer Hasselquist who said, "The nighthawk is very ravenous in Syria, and in the evenings, if the windows be left open, it flies into the house and kills infants, unless they are carefully watched; wherefore the women are much afraid of it."

All raptors can be very dangerous when defending themselves. Trying to capture and hold one could easily cause a person to be torn and severely scratched by their sharp talons. The nighthawk has unique characteristics and can speak to us from a prophetic perspective about prayer that operates covertly, faith that flies beneath the radar avoiding the detection of doubt, and deep fellowship with God that takes place in the night. There is debate among ornithologists (those who study birds) as to what *tachmas* or "nighthawk" is in our modern time. Substantial changes have taken place with the animal life of Israel over the past thousand years. Lions and bears have completely disappeared, having been hunted out and eliminated by the Crusaders around the thirteenth century. Other animals have also vanished off the regional scene due in part to Israel's rapid pace of human development over the last one hundred fifty years. These changes make it difficult to pinpoint with accuracy certain animals and birds mentioned in the Bible. Some think the biblical nighthawk could refer to an owl, or the nightjar, while others feel it is today's version of what is currently identified as the nighthawk. It is most likely that the biblical nighthawk went extinct centuries ago as the old-time eyewitness descriptions of this bird identify it as having been much larger and more aggressive in nature than the bird now identified as the nighthawk. The more modern, scaled-down version that carries the same name today still operates with a stealth method, allowing the legend of the nighthawk to live on.

The nighthawk has no nest but lays its eggs often in a sandy place or on flat gravel roofs. When their young are hatched they are so well camouflaged that they're hard to find. Even the adults seem to have the ability to vanish as soon as they land on the ground. These beautiful birds fly in graceful loops. When they pass quietly by you can see their white patches out past the bend of each wing.

Nighthawks eat mainly insects, which is a better option than small children, as mentioned earlier. Their diet consists of ants, wasps, beetles, moths, bugs, flies, crickets, grasshoppers, termites, and other insects as well. Nighthawks eat at dusk, dawn, even at night, and especially on moonlit nights. It is considered to be a nocturnal bird, meaning that much of its activity takes place at night. New realms of faith can be explored and developed through engaging in night missions with God, just like the nighthawk.

I believe it's good for us to all have some nighthawk qualities within us. There is a different anointing that flows when you get up to pray in the night. It's different from the late morning or evening times of prayer. Getting up in the nighttime to pray is never going to be noticed by others. It's a clandestine operation that is cloaked in divine secrecy. These "night missions" can greatly embolden your faith through hearing from God and receiving supernatural insight that God shares with you. Hearing from God always causes faith to come alive because the *rhema* word is charged with life-giving power.

For several years I experimented with flying on "night operations" before enlisting for regular duty. These missions proved to be so rewarding, but also so difficult to carry out. We all live in a physical body that requires sleep in order to remain healthy. It's never enjoyable to feel tired physically. There are techniques the Lord gives the nighthawk Christian to gain the needed sleep that is necessary to be healthy and have a sharp mind while still carrying out long-range night assignments.

Our Lord Jesus was the master of knowing how to grab the necessary shuteye, whether it was in the back of a boat while crossing to the other side of the Galilee or beneath the stars on a blanket in the Judean wilderness. Once you establish a rhythm and a pattern of praying at night, you soon form a routine, which helps it become easier to structure your time for sleep.

While the four gospels (Matthew, Mark, Luke, and John) offer us transparency into the life and ministry of Jesus, they are still very short books that cannot cover every detail of His movements. This is why we also study the Old Covenant to gain further insight into the life of Jesus, that we may imitate His practices.

> *The Sovereign Lord has given me a well-instructed tongue, to know the word that sustains the weary. He wakens me morning by morning, wakens my ear to listen like one being instructed* (Isaiah 50:4 NIV).

I love this verse. It's bursting with wisdom and revelation. Here we see that the Sovereign Lord (the heavenly Father) gave Me (Jesus) instruction. The Hebrew word for a person who was "instructed" is comparable to the English word "scholar". This endowment for learning requires an ear that is awakened. This verse contains valuable insight into the hidden devotional life of the Lord Jesus when He was on the earth. Notice it says, "He wakens me morning by morning." These were those night prayer sessions in which Jesus was personally taught by God the Father. The Hebrew day begins at sundown, not at the breaking of dawn. The morning period referred to here would be a time when it was most likely still dark outside before sunrise. When His ministry had begun it appears that what Jesus learned in the dark is what He would later teach in public during the day. Anyone who speaks in a scholarly and authoritative manner is someone who has been well taught. If Jesus needed to be taught, then we also need to enroll in the same process of higher learning.

The Scripture says, "He...wakens my ear." The word for "waken" in the Hebrew means to "stir up and arouse oneself." Many times the Holy Spirit wakes me up when it is time for me to pray in the middle of the night. Although I always set my alarm clock, many times He awakens me several minutes before my clock goes off. Jesus did not have an alarm clock, but He did have the Holy Spirit who helped awaken Jesus for His prayer sessions. A key emphasis I would like to point out in Isaiah 50:4 is the phrase "morning by morning." In other words, this speaks of being consistent with your attendance of the night school of the Spirit. You can't learn the material if you don't show up for class. In order for this to work you really must view your night sessions as being just as much of a requirement as going to a regular type of university and attending all of your classes throughout the course of a semester. The phrase "like one being instructed" refers to a disciple who is a learner or one who is being taught as in a classroom type of setting. We see the teaching and training revealed as well in the following verse.

> Sacrifice and offering You did not desire; my ears You have opened. Burnt offering and sin offering You did not require. Then I said, "Behold, I come; in the scroll of the book it is written of me. I delight to do Your will, O my God, and Your law is within my heart (Psalm 40:6–8).

This psalm clearly refers to the Messiah Jesus. Notice it says, "My ears You have opened." The idea is conveyed here that the ears were deaf before they were opened. There are some Christians who love the Lord but their ears are stopped up when it comes to understanding vital biblical principles and truths. The literal Hebrew says, "My ears You have dug out." The word for "dug" is the same Hebrew word used in the Bible to describe the digging out of a well or a sepulcher. Some scholars have suggested that this could possibly refer to the "boring through" of the outer circle or rim of the ear with an awl, which would point to the ceremonial act that bonds a slave to his master for the remainder of the master's life, even when the slave has the opportunity to be free. But here the idea of "digging" is different and conveys the meaning of "hollowing out, digging, and excavating" and of "making a passage through." This is the Holy Spirit excavation of digging deep to remove all dirt, debris, or soulish material that could impair one's ability to spiritually hear accurately. When did this digging occur in the life of Jesus? It took place in the night school of the Spirit. No one inherently knows everything. We all learn through teaching, growth, and grace. If Jesus had to be taught and have His ears dug out, then we certainly will need similar ministry by the Holy Spirit as well, for we are not above our Master.

What did the "digging out" of the Lord's ears allow Him to hear? He heard and understood a key revelation of the will of God, which was that "burnt offering and sin offering You [the heavenly Father] did not require." What then would be required of the Lord Jesus? The answer is total obedience leading to death upon a cross. Again, through the opening of His ears Jesus heard (understood) that He would be the sin offering for humanity, a deep revelation that required Jesus to surrender His life to the will of God without being able to accept any alternative choices to avoid the coming pain and suffering. With open ears, what He heard staggered Him to His very core. How did He respond to what His ears heard?

*The Lord God has opened My ear; and **I was not rebellious, nor did I turn away**. I gave My back to those who struck Me, and My cheeks to those who plucked out the beard; I did not hide My face from shame and spitting* (Isaiah 50:5-6).

Despite knowing that He would be scourged, have His beard pulled out, be spat on, be reviled, carry the sins of the world upon His shoulders, be separated from the Father, and eventually be crucified, Jesus still was not rebellious nor did He turn away from what He heard concerning His heavenly assignment. God is speaking each day to us. When our spiritual ears are dug out we can be gently led by the Holy Spirit in all matters of life, even into areas where we may face great challenges but are nevertheless included in the plan that God has for our lives.

> *Now in the morning, having risen **a long while before daylight**, He went out and departed to a solitary place; and there He prayed* (Mark 1:35).

In the dark is where the nighthawk Christians earn their degree in the school that is known for charging the highest tuition. You may be thinking, "What is the tuition price?" The tuition is an hour or two of your sleep, your surrender of comfort, your sacrifice of getting out of the warm bed and sitting in a chair in the dark to commune with God. This requires an extraordinary level of discipline not only to get up in the middle of the night, but also to go to bed at a sufficient time the night before so that you have the ability to get up at 3:00 A.M. You are not bionic or superhuman. Your body requires sleep.

The Christian who stays up late watching endless hours of sports or news and finally goes to bed at 1:00 a.m. will be unable to respond to the demands of the night school. If you stay up late, you may try to get up in the night, but you will find that your body simply won't respond. You won't be able to focus in class because you are exhausted. You must treat your night classes with God as seriously as you would if you were going to a class at Harvard or Yale at 8:00 A.M. The spirit is willing but the flesh (body) is weak. You have to organize your life around your classes at night school. Regular attendance with very few absences is the name of the game here. You are one on one with the Master teacher and He expects your attention to be high. Each morning you learn something new, and each morning there is the receiving of personal instruction and guidance. The wisdom and knowledge dispensed is beyond anything you'll ever learn in a normal classroom-type setting.

You may be wondering why the tuition for this school is so high. When we look at the world's leading universities we clearly see that some stand head and shoulders above others. For example, Harvard University in Cambridge, Massachusetts, is currently considered to be America's hardest university to get into, having an acceptance rate that usually falls below 6 percent. That means that out of their 39,000-plus applicants who apply for admission only about 2,000 are accepted. Why do so many students strive to enter elite universities? Name recognition has a lot to do with it, knowing that graduating from an elite school gives tremendous favor to an individual in the eyes of a potential employer. But there must be a significant substance that is identifiable that supports the core quality of a university's brand or image. What separates elite universities from other good universities? The answer is in the caliber of their professors. The elite universities have the world's best teachers on board. They are the experts in their field, and they lead and set the global pace for others to follow. This is why the night school of the Spirit is the hardest school of higher education on the planet to get into. It's because the teaching is supernatural. Classes are taught by the Lord Himself at the most unusual time, often at three o'clock in the morning, and in the most unusual place—in the dark.

Some of the graduates of this school have gone on to flow in revival glory. Walter Beuttler, a prophet known for his unique teaching on the manifested presence of God, was used mightily of God in a revival that took place in 1951 at Eastern Bible Institute in Green Lane, Pennsylvania. Brother Beuttler was a Bible teacher at EBI for thirty-two years. Between the early 1950s and up until his passing away in 1974, his travels took him to over 100 nations. In the following quoted story taken from a message preached by Brother Beuttler in the 1960s, you can see an example of how he was required to be a nighthawk in order to receive the instructions necessary to guide a mighty outpouring of the Holy Spirit. This occurred at the Bible school with about 200 students in attendance. The move of the Spirit was very intense and it lasted for ten days. Brother Beuttler said:

> I had such sharp discernment, and that took waiting before the Lord every night from 2:30 sharp till chapel time at 8:00 A.M. I do not know whether I had breakfast or not, but I had to get dressed and shaved. Except for the absolute necessary things to get ready, all the time was spent in waiting, simply sitting in the conscious awareness of His presence.
>
> The revival lasted ten days, and every morning at 2:30 on the dot, the Lord would awaken me. I knew it was time to get up and stay up. Time passed, 3:30, 4:30, 5:30, 6:30, let's say 7:00. Then I had to go about, get dressed and get ready for school. It happened every night for ten days. During those times, the Lord would let me know what He was going to do in every single meeting, a meeting at a time. It's true.
>
> I would go to chapel and say, "Students, this morning is going to be washday." The Lord was collecting our laundry. You don't understand that, do you? He was dealing with things in the heart that needed cleansing.
>
> Or I would say in a meeting, "Today is going to be victory day," or "Today is going to be this day." I had a name

for every service. The Lord would give me what to speak on. He would give me who should sing a solo, and what they should sing. I had to get the song for them, or request what to sing. They were not allowed to choose their own. (Normally they were.) I would get it from the Lord and I would give it to them. The Lord even let me know what stanza not to sing, what stanza to skip.

Time and again the Lord would give me minute details, even in the meetings where I was to stop and let Him take over the meeting completely. I'd sit down and He'd carry on the meeting on His own.

In one place I missed the signal. I knew where I was to stop doing anything on my own, and somehow where I was to stop, I messed up and kept talking explaining to the students what the Lord was doing. After a while, our dean of women stood up and gave an utterance in prophecy, "O that thou would keep silent, then He would speak for this day is His day." She didn't know whom it was meant for, but I knew.

And I sat down, humiliated. For two hours I didn't say, "Boo." I said, "Lord, You took the meeting out of my hands. I'll not touch that meeting no matter what happens until You give it back again." He gave me the meeting back after two hours. You see the meeting went all morning long, sometimes way into the afternoon. We start at 8:00, usually it went till dinnertime or later, that's four hours or more. For two hours the Lord carried on in that meeting. It was marvelous. Then He gave me back the meeting and I could go on with it.

And the Lord would share those things during the night. Honestly folks, I had a complete program (so to speak) of what He was going to do. I think I had what Jesus talked about, "The Father worketh, and I work hitherto." [See John 5:17 KJV.] The Father let me know what He was going to do in the meeting, and all I had to do was cooperate with Him to get His work done. All this during the night from 2:30 until about 7:00, just sitting, sitting, waiting, waiting, worshiping on the inside, a spirit going up in communion, in worship, in adoration, in admiration hour upon hour, night after night.[1]

Brother Beuttler's story is a good example of someone who was willing to pay the tuition price for the night school of the Spirit. There's room in the class for you to enroll as a nighthawk. What happens during these night sessions? Earlier I noted that the night sessions have a different feel, a different anointing. What is this anointing? It is the teaching anointing. Who in their right mind would go to school at three o'clock in the morning? The nighthawk does. Perhaps that's why this bird is sandwiched in the Scripture between the owl (representing wisdom) and the cuckoo (slang for someone a little bit crazy).

> The owl, and the night hawk, and the cuckow (Deuteronomy 14:15 KJV).

The wise-owl Christian sees the potential for an unprecedented learning experience. The crazy cuckoo Christian is delirious enough to go to school in the middle of the night. God made the cuckoo; perhaps there's some cuckoo in all of us. It is a remarkable combination of wisdom and out-of-the-box quirkiness that when put together produces one whose ears have been awakened and deeply excavated.

If you have never tried flying as a nighthawk, I encourage you to give it a try. It produces an ability to sustain incredible faith for the supernatural and the miraculous in your daily life. Set your alarm, get up very quietly to not disturb others, spend time with the Lord in the night, and when finished get a few more hours of sleep before starting your work day. The Night School of the Spirit is now enrolling night-hawks. See you in flight!

NOTE

1. Walter Beuttler, "Waiting on the Lord," sermon. Transcribed by Reverend Pearl Ray of Harvest Age Ministries. Text available through Parousia Ministries, accessed September 10, 2016, http://www.wadetaylor.org/Articles%20by%20Others/Walter%20Buettler/PRAYER/Waiting%20on%20the%20Lord.html.

Chapter Six

THE PROGRESSIVE NATURE OF FAITH

*For I am not ashamed of the gospel of Christ, for it
is the power of God to salvation for everyone who
believes, for the Jew first and also for the Greek. For
in it the righteousness of God is revealed from **faith to
faith**; as it is written, "The just shall live by faith."*
—ROMANS 1:16-17

The more you study your Bible and read through it, the more you
see that our faith is in a gradual state of forward and progressive
momentum. For instance, you used your faith to call upon the
name of the Lord and thus received salvation in Christ along with
its benefits, which include forgiveness of sins and eternal life. Yet
you did not stop there but progressed in faith by joining a church
and becoming an active member. After some time, you most likely
went to a bookstore and purchased your own Bible; then perhaps
you began watching Christian television programs to learn more
from various teachers. As time moved on you possibly found yourself attending occasional Bible conferences to learn from different

ministers, so you didn't stay stagnant but progressed further in the Christian faith.

Faith in God is always practical and accomplishes its purpose, often through progressive small steps. Often we limit our ability to accomplish great things because we never take the first initial steps to go in the direction to start the journey. Some think, "Why start when there's no way it can even be done?" But faith says, "It does look impossible, but let's take the first initial steps in the right direction and trust God."

A former church property our ministry owned was densely surrounded by large red oak trees when we purchased it. Upon close inspection of these trees, it was discovered most were diseased and had severe rot issues. This was confirmed through the examinations of several tree arborists. The trees were also a liability by being so close to the church. They were old and needed to be brought down before they could be blown over in a storm. We decided to engage in a "faith project" and have them removed by a professional tree service company. What I mean by a "faith project" is that we did not have the extra money set aside in our church savings to tackle this project, so instead we would have to pray and use our faith for the needed funds.

As we announced this project to our church family and ministry partners, the Lord's people gave and the money supernaturally came in to keep pace with each tree as it was cut down and removed. Some of these were excessively large trees around the age of 80 to 100 years. There would be extra costs involved because of their enormous size and their proximity to the church building. We had one particular pine tree that was fifty feet tall and actually leaned directly over the fellowship hall—it reminded me of the Leaning Tower of Pisa. But in faith we moved forward on this project. Slowly the smaller sized trees began to come down first, and then the giant ones began to fall as we moved forward.

Today, there are no longer any trees around the church build-ing. However, if we had not stepped out in faith nothing would have changed and the problem would still be around. People would still be tripping or rolling their ankles on the hundreds of acorns that would fall upon the sidewalks every Sunday morning. When the largest oak tree was cut down piece by piece, we discovered that the inside trunk of the tree was completely hollow from the top of the tree to the very bottom. The tree cutter expressed astonishment and said that it seemed to be miraculous that it had not yet fallen over. If it had fallen over it could have come down against the church building or upon somebody if they were standing or parked beneath it. But step by step, tree by tree, we gained the overall victory. Progressive faith can make a project look easy. Yet the truth is that in the total project there were many small steps that were taken that eventually helped get us to the finish line.

We are transported from faith to faith. This is how we live. This is how we function in the eternal kingdom of God. Our Scripture verse of going from "faith to faith" comes from the letter that Paul wrote to the church in Rome. There is a popular saying that is often quoted today among people, which is, "Rome was not built in a day." In other words, we may look and marvel at the grandeur or complexity of a project and wonder how something so imposing could have been built. I think we can better comprehend this when we consider the answer to the proverbial question of, "How do you eat an elephant?" The correct answer is, "One bite at a time." When we step out in faith and go step by step so that our faith is not reaching beyond its capacity of what it can sustain, then we are sure to complete our mission.

As we develop this principle, consider that each New Year count-less people make resolutions to lose weight. But unless a person is willing to change their eating habits and start eating healthy and enroll some form of exercise into their life then the goal of weight loss will once again be out of reach. People sometimes ask themselves the question, "How did I get so overweight?" The answer is, "One bite at a time." As we mentioned, Rome wasn't built overnight, and if the city were to be disassembled it would not be taken apart overnight either. If a person has reached an unhealthy weight, then it took time to get into that position. It will also take some time to lose the weight in a progressive way. But you have to start somewhere, so by faith you begin with a plan of action and trust God for His grace to carry you through each day. All you have to do is go one day at a time. Break it down into small steps and it is easier to visualize doing it. Have a goal for each day, each week, a three-month goal, and a one-year target.

Each day that you accomplish your daily goal you become stronger. If you are spending extra time seeking the Lord with fasting and prayer, then mentally focus on going one day at a time. Some people consider a forty-day fast to be an unthinkable feat or an act of supernatural ability. While it is an act that requires the marvelous grace of God to carry out effectively, it is not an impossible endeavor. I have spoken to quite a few people over the years who began a short one- or three-day fast and experienced the grace of God to keep going. They simply went one day at a time without ever originally intending to do an extended fast. Yet before they knew it they were at ten days, then twenty-one days. Feeling blessed within their hearts they chose to carry on to thirty days, with some even reaching forty days.

This is moving from faith to faith. You reach a certain level and you think to yourself, "I'm going to push a little further because I sense the grace of God." This is exactly what happened to my assistant, Brother Michael, during a recent twenty-one-day juice fast that I started in the month of January. He tagged along with me drinking various fruit juices, and eventually we reached the summit of day twenty-one. It was a stepping off point for me because I had fulfilled my commitment to the Lord, but Michael felt a grace to keep on going. By God's abundant grace he eventually reached the conclusion of the fortieth day, having gone the entire duration with no food and drinking primarily orange juice. He has no seminary training. He has never gone to a formal Bible school. He doesn't know Greek or Hebrew. He makes his living working on a film crew in the movie industry. Anyone can have a deep walk with God; you don't have to be called into the ministry to go on spiritual ventures. Today he is flourishing in every facet of his life; the favor of God is clearly resting upon him.

You will never accomplish your full purpose in life if you do not exercise your God-given faith and start moving toward your destiny. When you do all you can in the natural to move forward, then the Lord will be waiting to meet you at each progressive level to take you onward. Often it may require God's miraculous intervention for you to progress forward in your path. But miracles come in correspondence with a faith that refuses to procrastinate but is active in making daily progress.

While spending time in prayer one day, I heard the Lord ask, "Where would you like to go with your faith?" Your faith has a destination. Some places may seem out of reach or inaccessible, but you are supposed to eventually arrive there, and by His grace you certainly will. Meditate on where you would like to be five years, even ten years from now. Dream with God. Often the Lord will encourage us by showing us a glimpse of the good things He has in store for us. However, He will not reveal everything up front because it would overwhelm us.

Your future that lies before you includes generational blessings. The plan of God will always extend through you to touch the lives of others and make their life sweeter. Your faith is carrying you into the reality of the manifested promises of God. You may not see it all now, but as you move forward always bear in mind that it is the accomplishing of the little things that eventually produce the sum total of a big and glorious result.

In the Bible we read the story of the four men who were lepers and in a destitute condition (see 2 Kings 7:1–20). King Ben-Hadad of Syria besieged Samaria (the capital of Israel's Northern Kingdom), and this produced a severe famine in the Jewish land. People were literally starving to death. The lepers were already on the bottom of the barrel even before the famine took place. While discussing their dire condition they said to one another a statement that has now become an eternal classic, "Why are we just sitting here waiting to die?" They agreed that it was better to try something drastic instead of doing nothing, so they got up and started walking toward the enemy camp of the Syrians. In the same manner, you must stir yourself up to overcome discouragement and despair. No matter what your condition is you must remember that Jesus said, "I will never leave you nor forsake you."

What the leprous men did not know was that as they walked forward the Lord caused the camp of the Syrians to hear the noise of a great army. The Syrian soldiers reasoned among themselves that the king of Israel must have hired the Hittites and Egyptians to attack them. The Syrians were struck with fear, became delusional, and immediately fled in a panic while leaving behind all they had accumulated—their tents, horses, donkeys, silver, gold, clothing, and even their weapons. It seems somewhat strange that the soldiers had so much gold and silver. Soldiers don't normally wear luxury items such as gold Rolex watches, gold necklaces, and silver rings. This would appear to be a setup from the Lord to transfer material assets into the hands of the people of God.

Like the four lepers, your forward progress, even if it is small steps, is an act of faith that moves the hand of God to go before you and make a way where there currently is no way. You don't need to focus on how

God is going to work a miracle, but rather keep your concentration on putting one foot in front of the other. God is well able to fulfill His side of the deal by working miracles. What often happens when we stay focused and are operating in steady faith is that God then comes along and does something wonderful that was even beyond what we were hoping for. The four lepers were going to the Syrians to surrender and hopefully have their lives spared and maybe be thrown a few pieces of stale bread. They had no idea that their small steps of faith would end up producing a miraculous sound that would release the power of God to scatter the enemy.

In the fullness of the plan of God we see that not only were the four lepers blessed with abundant provision and an eternal faith legacy, but also the Israelites were delivered from what appeared to be certain death. This story reveals to us that there is more at stake here than just your own personal blessing. God is counting on you to keep moving. You cannot afford to stop or slow down because the salvation and spiritual well-being of others is linked to the success of your walk of faith. You influence more people than you think. You encourage more people than you are aware of. The destiny of others is riding on your shoulders.

Quoting from the prophet Habakkuk, the apostle Paul told us that "the just shall live by faith" (Rom. 1:17). If a big assignment is before you, then start accomplishing it one step at a time. Whether it's a home remodel, a new landscape for your backyard, a dream to run for political office, or a divine longing to help share the gospel in places where it has not yet reached, it is all capable of being accomplished through progressive faith. Release your faith today and find a way to move forward with another step.

Chapter Seven

THE MAGNETISM OF FAITH TO WIN

Your faith works in a process similar to that of a magnet. Magnetism occurs when subatomic particles line up in a certain way when they encounter an electric charge. Miracles occur when movements and activities you can't always see or track with the physical eye line up in the right order when they are exposed to the magnetic charge of faith. Magnets can be found everywhere—our earphones, cars, computers, and the little souvenir magnets on our refrigerator doors. The earth itself is a giant magnet, and even has its own magnetic field that stretches far into space. If you view your faith as a magnet and use it accordingly, you will be able to attract the distant desires of your heart toward you through the transcendent power of God.

We are learning more about magnets through ongoing research and deeply funded scientific study. In some ways magnets almost seem miraculous with their effect upon certain objects. Japanese maglev (short for magnetic levitation) trains float along through the air at speeds that are well over three hundred miles per hour. These high-speed trains have no wheels, axles, or bearings, so there's no friction, which allows the trains to go faster than other trains while maintaining a smooth and comfortable ride. It's amazing to see something so large suspended in the air and pushed and pulled forward by an invisible magnetic current. Just as science is tapping into the power of magnets, we can access new dimensions of blessing through the usage of faith.

A spiritual law in the Scripture directs us to "walk by faith and not by sight." With a maglev train you can't see what's actually causing it to float, nor can you see how it's moving because the train doesn't have an engine. But it's not necessary to understand the physics of magnetism in order to purchase a ticket and travel on this train. Similarly, the science of faith requires us to first take God at His word (purchase the ticket), and then second we will see the promised results (we get to ride on the train). We see this spiritual law clearly outlined in the teachings of the Lord Jesus, although not all followed the procedure of faith and therefore some missed the train. In the fourth chapter of Luke's gospel, Jesus was speaking to the Jews in His hometown of Nazareth. The local Jews wanted to see Jesus do the same type of miracles He had done in other cities. Jesus could not replicate the same kind of miracles in Nazareth because of the unbelief of the people. He explained this to them by illustrating from God's Word why their faith was necessary for them to receive their own personal miracle. He also emphasized the role they needed to play in order to be the recipient of a miracle. In other words, the working of miracles was not simply a random act Jesus performed, but was most often a direct response in correlation with the faith of the person in need. In the fourth chapter of Luke's gospel, Jesus clearly points out that unmet needs at times can be directly linked to unbelief concerning the promises of God.

> *But I tell you truly, many widows were in Israel in the days of Elijah, when the heaven was shut up three years and six months, and there was a great famine throughout all the land; but to none of them was Elijah sent except to*

Zarephath, in the region of Sidon, to a woman who was a widow (Luke 4:25-26).

Jesus referred to there being "many" widows, which leads us to ponder—how many is "many"? I don't think two hundred widows would be classified as "many." Perhaps three thousand or more would be, but it would have to be a large number of widows to be considered "many." These weren't normal widows, however. These were Jewish widows who "were in Israel." This is more than a geographic pin-pointer of where they lived, but more accurately refers to the truth that they were the descendants of Abraham and thus qualified for full covenant benefits. These were the widows who knew the Torah and the promises of God, yet they were suffering and perishing just like the heathen and idolatrous widows from the nations that surrounded them. Out of all these widows in this Middle Eastern region who faced starvation and thirst due to the effects of the famine, only one received divine deliverance. Who was the widow who received?

She was a gentile widow from Zarephath, in the region of Sidon. Zarephath was a Phoenician seaport lying on the Mediterranean coast between Sidon and Tyre. Today, Zarephath lies beneath the modern fishing village of Sarafand, in Lebanon. Dr. James Pritchard of the University of Pennsylvania discovered the city in 1970, and in 1972 uncovered in Zarephath the first Phoenician temple found in Lebanon, along with a figurine of Ashtoreth, the fertility goddess of the Phoenicians. The widow Jesus refers to was not Jewish. She had no covenant rights, lived in a heathen idolatrous culture, yet she received a miracle from God while the Israeli widows were dying in anguish.

When the Jews in Nazareth heard Jesus say this, their tempers began to boil because it was an indictment of their sin of unbelief. Jesus was bringing the full force of two key revelations to them that they refused to accept. Of these two revelations, the first dealt with salvation through Him for all the nations of the world, not just for the Jews, and the second key teaching He presented was that God responds to faith, not to need, regardless of who you are.

The Jews took great pride in their ancestry and their identification with Abraham as their father of the faith. But here Jesus points out the reason why the Jewish widows during Elijah's day did not receive God's intervention—it was because not one Jewish widow trusted God to deliver them from the effects of the famine. God did, however, find a Gentile widow who had faith for deliverance from the famine's cruel effects. Her faith was tested to the utmost limit, but she continued to place her trust in Jehovah God. Because of this God sent his choice servant, the prophet Elijah, to her to be a means of deliverance. Her magnetic faith drew the prophet away from his country and into a foreign land. Of course, when Elijah showed up the first thing he did was receive an offering from an impoverished old woman. You can only imagine how the twisted worldly media would exploit this story today. Yet God's method of receiving through faith along with the principles of sowing and reaping does not change to suit the opinions of men.

Jesus continued to emphasize the necessity for specific faith in order to move the hand of God by sharing another biblical illustration. This time He mentioned the prophet Elisha. The Lord pointed out that there were many lepers in Israel in the time of Elisha and none of them were cleansed except a Gentile from a neighboring country, Naaman the Syrian. Just as there were thousands of suffering Jewish widows during the previous famine, there certainly must have been thousands of suffering Jewish lepers. The only leper who received divine healing from his disease was Naaman. Not a single Jewish leper was healed. This is because Naaman was the only person God could find who had specific faith that God could heal him of his leprosy. When Jesus told this story, it caused the Jews in Nazareth to go full tilt. They exploded in rage, knowing that His teaching unmasked their religious façade that guised their unbelief and doubt. They actually tried to throw Jesus over a cliff because He told them the truth.

Sometimes there are Christians who still have the same mind-set as the Jews did in Nazareth during Jesus' day. They think just because they are a Christian, go to church, pray, and sing in the choir that God will automatically cause every divine promise to somehow just float into their lives. These dear saints use their faith for salvation but fail to apply it to remove various complications and dilemmas out of their lives. Other Christians have mind-sets that think once they are saved they then have to trudge through life defeated by the difficulties and misfortunes of this world. But our faith is the victory that overcomes the world.

Faith produces a lifestyle of winning. Once when preparing to preach a New Year's Eve message, I waited on the Lord all day at the church in prayer. After praying for hours I lay down on the floor to rest a little bit. Lying there I said, "Lord, I know You would like to share a word of encouragement with Your people. What would You say to them?" As I lay there on the floor, I looked up and could see underneath the bottom of the green church chair that I had placed my Bible on. There, on the underside of the chair was a note attached that said "WINNER!" We had purchased these chairs used, but they were in very good condition when we acquired them. Obviously, there must have been a raffle or some sort of random drawing held in a conference room in a former time in which someone sitting in that chair was selected to be the winner of a prize. I checked all of the other chairs, but the "winner" note was only placed on one single chair. Faith helps you to win in life. It's time for all of your losses to be stopped. God has selected you to be a winner, and He is launching you on a winning streak unlike anything you've ever experienced before. You have been divinely chosen to sit in the seat of winning. Always walk in a frame of mind of being a winner.

It is the spirit of faith that carries you to a place where failure is not an option and you tenaciously refuse to quit. God expects us to progress from faith to faith, glory to glory, strength to strength, and thus enjoy ongoing promotion into higher levels of our natural and spiritual lives. Our faith is not only to be used for salvation but can also be applied to receive divine healing (such as Naaman the leper) and even financial provision (as seen with Elijah and the starving widow). God doesn't change His principles just because we are born again or volunteer to work in the church. If we fail to apply our faith to possess the promises God speaks to us, then we risk falling into a perpetual cycle of having unmet needs and unfulfilled desires.

As you exercise your faith you are drawing the needed miracle closer and closer into your life with a heavenly magnetic pull. Demeaning accusations against God and getting upset at God because it's "not happening fast enough" are dark places of unbelief to steer away from. Don't let others in their weakness pull you into joining them in speaking wrong of the Lord. Minister with mercy and compassion to others and always be mindful of the goodness of the Lord. Even if God has to send someone from another country to minister personally to you, He will do so if needed. God will not let you down. Your specific faith in His promise to you will be manifested as you continue to trust Him and expect your miracle to come forth. Each day you are boldly possessing every blessing God has intended for you to receive.

In life we encounter many obstacles that are excellent opportunities for us to use our faith and turn negatives into positives. Years back, my ministry was given a five-acre plot of vacant land as a donation. It was a beautiful piece of property, but after it was donated I soon discovered that it had a hitch attached that would prove a real challenge to resolve. The land was located in a rural mountain subdivision. It was on the back side of a mountain so it was very peaceful and quiet, possessing lots of deer and wild turkey; oak, pine, and walnut trees abounded—the perfect place to build a prayer or retreat cabin. In order to build a home on the property, the soil would have to first pass a percolation test. This is necessary when putting in a septic system for a home where there is no existing municipal sewer system. Soil that percolates properly will allow the excess waste water from the septic tank, which is released through the perforated plastic pipes in the "leach field," to drain away properly. In most cases properties can easily pass a perc test when the soil has higher concentrations of sand. This is due to sand being able to absorb water at a faster rate than silt or clay. Sand is good at the beach, but on the side of a mountain location there's usually not too much to be found.

In order to perform the soil percolation test, we had several holes dug with an excavator so that the county health department soil inspector could come and analyze the soil. I was confident the soil would easily pass inspection because there were homes scattered across the mountain that had each successfully received their permit. Once the inspector arrived, he pulled out his kit and carefully began checking the soil with his hands. After about twenty minutes he informed me that the soil from the sample holes did not pass the required standards. He suggested that more holes be dug from various areas of the property to see if there could possibly be other options for where to place the septic system. Once again, about a week later, an excavator was brought out and holes were dug all over the property. Most of the holes were large enough and deep enough for the inspector to climb down into. My dream ministry property began to look somewhat like the surface of the moon with craters everywhere.

Eventually, the same county inspector arrived back to my property. Before he came, a local general contractor warned me about this particular inspector, making known to me that this inspector was the bane of all the local home builders. When the contractor heard that this same inspector was assigned to do my soil test he expressed grave concern, knowing that I would be in for some real trouble. He said all the general contractors dreaded when this inspector showed up because of his unrealistic standards that he insisted be met. This inspector was known throughout the county for being excessively over cautious in all his tests, making it almost impossible for any land to pass unless it met and even exceeded ideal textbook conditions. But all of the other soil inspectors understood that in the real world there are very few textbook perfect conditions. They knew that all mountains are composed primarily of rock and you're not going to have perfect sandy soil at high elevations. Nevertheless I was stuck with him and there was nothing I could do but pray and hope to get through it.

Upon his arrival he began to check the newly dug holes, going from one to the other without speaking, scrutinizing every detail of the dirt, marking off small questionnaire boxes on several papers attached to a brown clipboard, moving slowly and methodically with textbook precision, and after thirty minutes he stoically informed me that not a single hole had passed his inspection. Upon asking him how he reached this conclusion, he simply said my land had too much stone in the soil. I thought it might help to remind him that the next local mountain a few miles away was literally called Stone Mountain, and yet it had hundreds of houses built on it. The locals who lived in the mountains knew it had stonier soil than our mountain, hence its name. But I also knew he had lived here in this county all of his life so he was aware of that, and I didn't want to be argumentative. I was handed another failing report.

Seeing that I was in a predicament of owning a piece of land that potentially could never have a livable structure built upon it, I asked the inspector if there was anyone "higher up on the chain of com-mand" at the health department who could review my situation. The only person higher up was his boss who oversaw all inspectors. He agreed to come out and offer his verdict. One week went by and the inspector along with the department head met me on my property. The department head was wearing a pair of dress slacks and very nice dress shoes, which I thought was odd to walk through the forest with, especially when it had rained the night before. I had the distinct feeling that he didn't get out of the office too much, nor did he do any real field work. He jumped down into the first hole that was deeper than his waist, thinking it was dry. The moment he touched the ground, his fancy, shiny shoes sunk down into about six inches of thick, dirty brown mud. He endeavored to behave in a professional demeanor, but I could tell the rest of the brief time he was there that he was miserable and just wanted to leave, get back to his indoor office, and get out of those muddy shoes. Within just a few minutes after arriving, he quickly expressed to me his agreement with his coworker's opinion, that the soil was not suitable for the installation of a septic system. They were back in the truck and gone faster than you could say, "Strike three, you're out!"

Indeed, all my attempts had struck out. I thought, "Lord, why would You bless the ministry with a beautiful piece of property that has no value because it can't be built on?" I went and sat down on a large rock on the property and pondered my situation. I prayed for about an hour and felt encouraged by the Holy Spirit. Perhaps the Lord knew of a solution that I was not yet aware of. The next day, I got on the phone and called the soil inspector who came out the previous three times. Refusing to throw in the towel, I inquired of him if he could offer any alternative plan. He did mention one complex option, such as pumping the waste water and sewage uphill far from the home site with an expensive pump and elaborate piping system. But this would cost tens of thousands of dollars, and he agreed the option presented didn't make sense for my building purposes.

I thanked him for his time and just before we hung up he threw me a ray of hope. He said, "I noticed that just below the proposed area where you planned to install the septic system there is a large rock strata that runs all the way through that field. If you can get me one good hole in that field I will pass your inspection. But I don't think that you can because it appears to be solid granite all the way through." I knew exactly the steeply sloped field he was referring to. Because I had walked over this field many times when clearing some of the property, I was aware that there did appear to be an uninterrupted vein of wide and deep granite. I thanked him and told him that he would hear back from me soon.

With a renewed determination to win, I met on the property the following morning with two local guys who had been sent to help me out. A neighbor had heard of my predicament, and in his kindness he sent these two men who were "specialists" in solving backwoods-type problems. This is the miracle of the magnetism of faith. By trusting in God and refusing to quit a door of favor opened for me, and God sent the exact help I needed.

There on the side of the mountain, meeting me at 6:30 in the morning were Bucky and Johnny. Bucky was known throughout the community as the man who could fix what others wouldn't even want to attempt to fix. Once I saw Bucky climb to the top of a thirty-foot ladder to separate a large tree that got hung up with another tree when falling due to a storm. He stood at the very top rung of the ladder with a chain-saw and began to cut the tree at the point of where it was jammed. With no harness, no safety goggles, and no gloves, he fully extended his right arm with the chain saw cutting at full power, all while dangling on the extreme side of the ladder with sawdust spewing into his eyes. Just before the tree snapped and freed itself, Bucky scrambled down the ladder and jumped back. In less than one second the damaged tree fractured and threw the supporting ladder that Bucky had just been standing on through the air as if it were a toothpick. If he had not stepped off at the exact moment that he did, then the tree would have thrown him at least forty or fifty feet. But I saw Bucky do stuff like this all the time and never get hurt. He had an uncanny instinct, a sixth sense you might call it, that he had developed from living in the woods that showed him when and when not to do a certain thing.

Yes, Bucky was a backwoods man. He was in his late thirties and was in excellent physical condition. Strong, wiry, and ripped with muscle, his persona was expressed through hard work and a willingness to never quit a job until it was completely finished and done the right way. You wouldn't find Bucky in church, but he was a great guy to be around. He had been a professional logger who eventually started his own freelance business of being a jack of all trades, fixing problems for people who lived out in the rural mountains. Of course, his concept of being a "real man" insisted on the necessity of driving the most rugged pickup truck that was possible to buy. One day while driving on the back side of the mountain on a narrow dirt road, I encountered Bucky when he had just upgraded to the newest model pickup truck. He was so excited when he saw me. Sticking his head out of the window with a big smile on his face, he said, "Hey Steven, how do ya' like my truck?"

I replied, "It's nice, I like the color" (which was black).

Holding up his hands to form a large circle he said, "The drive-shaft on this thang is this big!"

I said, "That's pretty cool."

But Bucky wasn't satisfied with my low sense of appreciation for something as important as a driveshaft. With pure backwoods sincerity he said, "Why don't ya' crawl under the truck and see it. It really is amazun'!"

"That's OK, Bucky," I said. "I'm sure it's just as big as you say it is." I was on my way to the church office to do some work, but Bucky so wanted me to get out of my vehicle and crawl with him on the dirt beneath his new truck to look up and see the glorious driveshaft. We all have different forms of what qualifies as personal happiness, don't we?

It was 6:30 in the morning, and I was happy to see Bucky and Johnny. The sun was just rising over the eastern horizon. The temperature was brisk, hovering around 28 degrees Fahrenheit. A thin blanket of frost lay upon the leaves of the forest floor. We could see our breath as we exhaled in the cold mountain air, as we discussed our game plan to find a hole somewhere through the rock strata that lay below where our potential septic field would be. Bucky was edgy, ready to get started. He had been up since 4:00 and he only felt comfortable when doing something. Neighbors had told me that the most Bucky ever slept was four hours per night. He constantly had work on his mind. Johnny, who was in his sixties, moved at a slower pace, being more thoughtful in his actions. But Bucky only had one gear, and that was full speed ahead.

An assortment of digging tools were carried to the site for us to try and find a way through the rock. Bucky grabbed a full-sized pickaxe, the type that gold prospectors would have used back in the olden days. With blood flowing through his veins and the carbohydrates of a full-course Southern breakfast energizing him, he hoisted the pickaxe overhead and held it high. The morning sun shone brightly upon the sharp metal axe, making it appear to be on fire. It was an epic moment, as he seemed to be Herculean in nature, truly living up to his legendary mountain-man reputation. Then, with tremendous velocity Bucky swung the axe downward to strike the ground. But as he did so, there was a problem. Perhaps he should have warmed up a little bit more before starting. Because as he swung he appeared to slightly loose his balance on the steep mountain incline, causing him to miss the ground, and he instead drove the pickaxe directly into his shin!

Bucky jumped all over that property, but never did he shed one tear, nor did he scream or shout out loud, although he did mutter something that sounded like speaking in tongues. Realizing the severity of the situation, I asked Bucky if he was OK. His only response was to nod "yes" and grab his fallen pickaxe from the ground and begin to dig furiously. Johnny and I immediately joined in on the work and soon an hour passed without us having any success. Everywhere we dug there was nothing but solid rock beneath the one inch of topsoil and leaves, just as the soil inspector had said. Soaked with sweat, we removed our outer layers of clothing and decided we must push on. Shovels, metal rods, axes, hoes, and all sorts of implements were tried in an effort to find a path through the rock. But it was no use—the rock strata ran wide and deep. Beginning to tire, we stopped to sit down. Bucky said, "Steven, it's like beatin' a dead horse. Nothin' we do is workin'." For about thirty seconds we all sat there silently. There was nothing else to be tried; unless God intervened my hopes for the development of this property would end at this point. Suddenly, Bucky seemed to be hit with a spark of genius. Quickly standing up he said, "Let's try that spot right over there!"

Grabbing his axe he approached a tiny place that neither three of us had yet explored. As he swung his axe downward, it instantly sank into soft soil upon contact with the ground. Bucky dropped to his knees and dug the hole deeper with his own hand. After reaching a depth of two feet Bucky exclaimed, "Don't touch the hole any further. This will pass inspection!"

Three days later, the soil inspector came out, took one look at the hole, and said, "You pass!" I received my official permit in the mail one week later. Glory to God. The remarkable thing about it was that our former holes were huge, some of them being five feet wide and four feet deep with enough room for four men to stand in. But this hole was only five inches wide and just two feet deep and was so skinny you could only get one hand down into it. That property had a special destiny upon it that unfolded more clearly to my understanding a few years later. If I had quit and lost faith, then a future blessing would have been compromised.

Faith pulls toward you the things you need to succeed. Faith functions with invisible divine magnetism, attracting favor, miracles, healing, the right relationships, the needed friends and resources, and new opportunities into your life. God never said that possessing our promised land would be easy. We are admonished to fight the good fight of faith. If you will trust God, then the help you need will somehow find you. God sent Bucky and Johnny to me; He may need to send someone to you as well. God will see that whatever you need to be a winner is always supplied. Expect it, and praise God for it, because it's on the way now!

Chapter Eight

FAITH FOR ANSWERED PRAYERS

*Now this is the confidence that we have in Him, that if
we ask anything according to His will, He hears us. And
if we know that He hears us, whatever we ask, we know
that we have the petitions that we have asked of Him.*
—1 JOHN 5:14-15

Over the years I have had the Lord answer some of my prayers that
from the natural viewpoint seemed impossible to fulfill, yet they were
answered through the miraculous power of God. In contrast, other
prayers that I thought would be much easier for God to answer never
got checked off of the list as being accomplished. Why are there fluc-
tuations in receiving answers to prayer? We would all agree that there
is nothing too difficult for the Lord. Even our largest requests would
not strain God in the slightest amount. His infinite ability, resources,
and power could never be exhausted. He can very easily supply every
request we present whether great or small. So, why are some prayers
answered and others are not?

Faith can never function beyond the will of God. Our prayers
and our faith are interconnected. Those needs or desires that we are
exercising our faith for must be in agreement with the will of God for

our lives. Likewise, what we ask for in prayer needs to be in harmony with God's plan for us. There are some things that God will bless and other things that He won't. We need to follow the guidelines of God's Word along with the inner witness of the Holy Spirit in these areas. God may give a thumbs-up approval for a person to do a certain thing, but that doesn't automatically mean that God endorses another person to do it. What is God's design for one may not be His strategy for another. Our prayers must be separated between that which is soulish in nature and that which purely emanates from our inner man, our born-again spirit. It brings tremendous confidence to attach your faith to something that you and God are both in unison about.

Prayer has to be played within the boundaries of the game. Of course, prayer is not actually a game, but I would like to use this wording simply as an illustration to help you see that prayer has certain rules. Just as basketball and football have rules that govern how their respective sports are played, there are also rules that must be followed in order for God to answer our prayers. For instance, in basketball you are not allowed to carry the ball; rather, you must dribble the ball when moving. If a person violates that rule, then they are called for "traveling" and the ball must be turned over to the opposing team. You can't win in sports if you don't follow the rules of that sport. You can't receive answers to prayer if you don't follow the rules that God established to govern prayer.

God is not obligated to answer unscriptural prayer. There is a certain section to the prayer mentioned by John that we love, and there's another part attached to it (a major rule) that we often skip over. The first part is wonderful and reveals that we can "ask anything." The confident ability to ask God for anything is breathtaking in its scope and reach. It's like being handed a blank check, given a pen, and left with the freedom to fill in the check with whatever amount we choose. But we must consider the balancing factor of the rule of prayer, which is that the prayer must be "according to His will." What if the prayer is sincere, persistent, well-meaning, but still out of God's will? What is the referee's call when a football player catches the ball but he did so out of bounds? No matter how much you plead your case with the referee or God, if your prayer is out of bounds (not His will for your life) then your prayer will not be answered.

Technically, a prayer not in harmony with the will of God is a prayer that God will not even hear. The Scripture said "that if we ask anything according to His will, He hears us." The reverse aspect of that truth would be, "If we ask anything *not* according to His will, He *doesn't* hear us." That's sobering. Some Christians labor in prayer over certain requests that God refuses to listen to. If God isn't paying any attention to our prayers, then we need to abandon false assignments and find out what He will respond to. It is possible for a Christian to be very strong in their willpower and determination when presenting their request to God. These are noble qualities, but our inner drive and our mental tenacity must always be willing to defer to the will of God.

Have you ever seen a professional athlete get upset with the referee because the athlete didn't agree with the ref's call? Yet the entire play is reviewed on a giant screen for everyone in the stadium to see, including the athlete, and the replay shows that the referee was correct. However, the athlete is still visibly displeased because of the denial of his personal objective. The referee or umpire is the higher authority, and it is his job to enforce the rules, which are fair to all players (or prayers). If our petition does not put a smile on God's face, then we should relinquish it peacefully.

> *Then I pleaded with the Lord at that time, saying: "...I pray, let me cross over and see the good land beyond the Jordan, those pleasant mountains, and Lebanon." ...So the Lord said to me: "Enough of that! Speak no more to Me of this matter"* (Deuteronomy 3:23, 25-26).

You would be hard pressed to find anyone with a stronger iron will and grit than Moses. But his deeply emotional request was considered by the Lord to be "out of bounds" and the supplication was firmly denied. Once, there was a certain venture that I wanted to become involved with. I presented it to the Lord in prayer and shared with Him my reasons for why I felt the request should be approved by Him. I felt like I had a pretty good case and really didn't see any reason why it would be turned down. The Lord did not immediately answer. In the meantime, I was leading our church into the beginning stages of a 21-day juice fast. A few days after the entire fast had been completed, I was sitting at home by myself just relaxing, reading a magazine, when I felt an inner urge to ask again concerning the venture I wanted to engage in. I simply said, "Lord, what do You think about that venture? I would like to have Your insight concerning it."

Calmly, I sensed the presence of the Lord draw near. I reached over and picked up the nearest Bible, which was a few feet away, randomly opened it, and let the pages fall where they may. Then a verse on that page seemed to be separated by the Holy Spirit, making it appear as if there was nothing else on the pages surrounding it. That one verse was all I could see. Slowly, I read the verse. It was so personal, so direct, and such an accurate response to my question that it could not have been more straightforward even if Jesus appeared before me and spoke it in Person. That verse had become God's living *rhema* word to me. The paraphrased essence of that verse basically told me, "No, do not do this or else it will be a distraction for you and turn your focus away from Me."

The presence of God hung in the air. I answered and said, "Lord, I'll never touch it again." At that point I let go of that desire and have stayed away from pursuing anything else in that direction.

Another point we should consider is while we pray according to His will and even strictly obey the rules of the game, the prayer outcome may still be unfavorable to us because of the limited boundaries of our authority. You can control your life, but you can't control someone else's life. If a person is under your authority, such as your young child who lives with you, then you have great influence in the direction and choices they select. Your prayers for them can be highly effective. As individuals we can choose to do the right thing, but others who are fully grown and independent have the freedom to make their own choices. Our prayers for them can be greatly influential, but they are still the ones who ultimately decide the fate of their lives. A person can choose to die in their sins and perish in the flames of hell if they want to, and God won't override their choice. That would be tragic, and it certainly wouldn't be the will of God because the Scripture tells us that God is not willing that any should perish but that all should come to repentance (see 2 Peter 3:9b).

God doesn't always get what He wants. That's a difficult statement for some, but it's a factual reality that becomes clearer the more we meditate on it. If God always received what He wanted, then everyone would be saved, the devil would be cast into the bottomless pit now for a thousand years, and we would move into the millennium reign of Christ. Yet untold thousands die every day in their sins, eternally lost and separated from God. If this is true concerning God, then we will also run into similar situations regarding our personal wishes and hopes that shape our prayers for America, Israel, the state we live in, our city, and elected government officials.

The reason for this fluctuation in prayer outcomes is because people can sovereignly choose what they want to do in life, even if their choice is willful disobedience. God has given you authority over your life, but not over the lives of others. We are not robots void of expression or inner conscience; we are all free to choose. God doesn't govern His kingdom by force or intimidation but respects our individual sovereignty. Anytime you sense intimidation to do a certain thing you can be assured that the fallen flesh nature of humanity is at work. God, the heavenly Father, does not compel anyone against their will to receive His Son Jesus to be their Lord and Savior. One particular religion that is followed by millions has a literal core belief that identifies all unbelievers as infidels, and they must be forced to "Convert or die!" This method of forced evangelism is rooted in the spiritually dead nature of unredeemed man. External conversions are not genuine conversions at all but are people responding out of fear of punishment for being a nonconformist.

Many of the various religions of the world are considered to be "peaceful" religions. They are peaceful until you begin to share Jesus with them, and then suddenly you see that they are not so peaceful after all. True peace can only be found in Jesus. Numerous times I have had Mormons and Jehovah's Witnesses come to my door to share their material with me to try and convert me to their beliefs. This doesn't bother me, and I always try to take time to speak heart to heart with them. Once, when speaking to a Mormon, I told him with kindness that I could not accept his literature because of conflicting beliefs I had between Christianity and Mormonism. Then I commended him for his sincerity to walk door to door, passing out tracts in the burning hot sun because of his desire to please God. I said to him, "God sees that you have a heart to know Him, and you are seeking after Him. He will bless you and reveal Himself to you more and more because you truly want to know Him." Upon hearing such kind words, he was literally stunned, and for a few seconds he didn't know what to say. Looking at him with a smile I asked, "You don't believe that Jesus is God, do you?"

"No, I do not believe that," he replied.

I said, "If you just get that simple problem worked out, you're going to be OK. You're a lot closer than you know to the kingdom of God." In our brief talk I think he caught a glimpse of the revelation that true conversion can never be to a system or an institution but must be to a *Person* whom you love. He thanked me for my words and headed on down the road, bypassing knocking on the doors of all the other homes next to me, and headed straight for his car and then drove away. Much of life is sowing seed so that a future harvest of someone's salvation can be reaped later at the moment when the mature golden grain is ready to be brought into the barns.

Another time I had a Jehovah's Witness evangelistic team hit my neighborhood in full force. Two by two they went, canvassing the area, knocking on every door, and passing out their free magazine and literature. A man and his wife along with all his young children came to my front porch area; through my window I saw the husband ascend up the stairs and ring my doorbell. I could tell that they were sending this particular family to me as their very best presentation of their religious values. The man was wearing a nice suit, while his wife and their four lovely children stood at the base of the steps endeavoring to present the perfect family image. It seemed so ideal, yet the whole picture was dreadfully wrong. As the husband knocked on my door I stepped outside on my porch to greet them—the temperature outside was 26 degrees Fahrenheit!

Immediately, the man began his brief memorized speech and offered me a free copy of their full-color magazine. I politely declined and shared with him that I couldn't accept the material because of conflicting beliefs that I could not validate in the Scriptures. He wanted to engage me in a theological dialogue, but I quickly switched the subject. Lowering my voice so that his wife and children could not hear what I was about to say, I then said to him, "Sir, you are only concerned about converting my soul in order to gain acceptance among your church leaders, whom you greatly esteem. You crave their recognition, and you do these extreme works such as going out in subfreezing weather to prove your zeal. But, my friend, look at your children. As we stand here they are visibly shivering and miserable because they are suffering in the cold. Your wife's face is almost completely blue because of the biting wind. Your religious works are very displeasing to God, and you can never gain heaven this way." When I said that, all of the blood seemed to drain from his face and he looked as white as a sheet. He went back down the steps (much faster than he had come up them) and gathered his family and quickly left. When the gift of discerning of spirits is in manifestation, it can supernaturally reveal the intentions of people's hearts. Nevertheless, it was another seed sown that I pray will one day produce a harvest of understanding in that man's life to pursue a real relationship with God and not a relationship to a very misguided religious system.

God has created man to rule and govern over his own life as a king. We are to function in this position beneath the exalted kingship of Jesus, who is King of kings and Lord of lords (see Rev. 19:16). You and I are the kings and lords over whom He is King and Lord. Jesus has great respect for the monarchial position in which you stand. He does not coerce His subjects but gently and patiently guides them into the knowledge of the truth. Prayer for others accelerates their grasping of the will of God and has a deep working effect. We are directed in the Scripture to pray for our government leaders even if we didn't vote for them or share the same worldview.

> *Therefore I exhort first of all that supplications, prayers, intercessions, and giving of thanks be made for all men, for kings and all who are in authority, that we may lead a quiet and peaceable life in all godliness and reverence. For this is good and acceptable in the sight of God our Savior* (1 Timothy 2:1–3).

When Paul wrote these words, Nero was the emperor of Rome. In July of AD 64, a great fire broke out in the city and lasted for six days, destroying ten of Rome's fourteen districts. Many historians suggest Nero had the fire started to destroy Rome so that he could build a new city named after himself. In order to shift blame from himself, Nero found it convenient to use as a scapegoat for the fire an obscure new religious group known as the "Christians." He had the Christians arrested, rounded up, and then fed to the lions and tigers in the Roman circus. Many were crucified. Others were burned to death at night on stakes to provide lighting for Nero's gardens, while he walked around and casually conversed with friends about sports, poetry, and the arts. Yes, Nero was a sick and twisted man. He was bisexual, vicious, cowardly, bipolar, extravagant, had two marriages to two men (one being a teen), was demon-possessed, and later in life fully deranged. He had a 103-foot-tall bronze statue built of himself and placed near the Colosseum. (Keep in mind that the Statue of Liberty is 111 feet tall.) His last words just before committing suicide were, "What an artist the world loses in me." It is in this context in which Paul admonished us to pray for our leaders with the intent that we would be able to live quiet and peaceful lives so that the gospel work may go forth unhindered to all the world.

If we don't pray, then things could be much worse than Nero, whose persecution and evil was regionally contained due to the limitations of the ancient world in which he lived. This is especially true in a day where numerous leaders who do not have biblical moral values have nuclear, chemical, and biological weapons at their disposal, thus affecting the lives of millions of people. Such leaders can also make life miserable for Christians and Jews, particularly as the Western world is becoming more pressured through the wicked spirit of political correctness that currently has a stronghold over North America and Europe. In democratic countries it's not just enough to pray, we must also vote. It always amazes me when I meet Christians in America who have never voted in an election to choose a governor for their state or to vote their choice for President. We must be the salt and light in the earth and do our best to see that leaders with biblical values are elected, or else we could end up with another Nero, even in America. Prayer can alter world history and will help shelter our leaders so they may experience alleviation from the spiritual hosts of wickedness in the upper atmosphere, who try to influence them to do things detrimental to the work of God and make the world a darker place.

When it comes to praying for our national leaders I am mindful of Saint Francis of Paola. Most people are familiar with Saint Francis of Assisi, but they haven't heard of his spiritual son who is named Saint Francis of Paola, Italy, who established nearly 500 monasteries and who was a major influence directly in the lives of seven popes and five kings. King Louis XI of France heard about this humble monk and requested that he come to France and pray for him to recover from a stroke that left him partially paralyzed and unable to speak properly. Francis did not want to go but was eventually directed by the Pope to leave behind Italy and his beloved friars in order to minister to the king. The hermit friar left Italy and headed to France to see Europe's most powerful ruler. Along with three of his hermit companions, Francis arrived in Tours, France, where in front of a large crowd King Louis fell on his knees, and with tears streaming down his face he begged Francis to heal him.

Much to the king's surprise, Francis did not pray for his healing. Rather, he constantly spoke to the king about the need for him to be concerned for his soul, which was of far greater importance than physical healing. Hundreds of people were healed through the anointed ministry of Francis, either through a word or a simple touch. But the main ministry of Francis was to prepare the king for his death. Thoughts of dying terrified the king, but Francis taught him regularly from the Scriptures, and just before he passed away the king received salvation through Jesus. King Louis died peacefully in the arms of

Francis. The king's son, Charles VIII, retained Francis to be his spiritual advisor. Francis was not just a spiritual giant, but also when asked he gave wisdom concerning politics that greatly aided King Charles in avoiding what appeared to be an almost certain civil war in France.

Francis lived a lifestyle of extreme severity in his fasting and mortifications. His only food was vegetables and fruit. The monastic order he established continues in existence today, where its followers still practice the same rules established by Francis of eating no meat, no fish, no eggs or dairy products, or any food derived from animals. Francis lived to the age of 91 before passing away—not bad for someone who lived in an era when the average life expectancy was in the high sixties at best for most people. Francis lived at the court of France for twenty-five years. When you read secular and historical accounts of King Louis and his son Charles, you see an example of kings in authority who struggled in their faith, and from all perspectives they looked like war mongrels—incompetent, insecure, greedy, lustful men who had no knowledge of God. But behind the scenes God sent Francis to mentor them, counsel them, and constantly pray for them. If many of their actions recorded in the annals of history reflect their poor choices, we then can only imagine how much more harm, pain, bad decisions, or suffering they would have caused without someone like Francis praying for them and speaking into their lives. Most of the world's leaders are not spiritual. In other words, they have no prayer life and they do not follow the Scriptures as their guideline in decision-making. This is why we must intercede for them in prayer so that they are divinely influenced to do good.

Months before the presidential elections of 2008, I spent much time praying and holding local church prayer meetings for our national election. It was deeply troubling to me that the moral foundations of the nation were being eroded away and would be further weakened if someone were elected who did not have biblical values and morals.

Just a few days before the election we had another prayer meeting with about twenty-five of us gathered together. In this meeting I sensed a great heaviness, as if our many prayers along with the prayers of hundreds of thousands of other conservative believers across America throughout the previous months had come up short. Just before the prayer meeting concluded I went into a vision. In the vision the Lord Jesus walked through the wall in front of me and came over to me where I was kneeling in prayer. I saw that He was wearing a white robe and had on brown sandals. He put His hand on my shoulder and looking down at me peacefully and with great sincerity said, "Thank you, for praying." He smiled warmly at me, and at the same time I could see from the look on his face an expression that indicated, "It's not going to be the way you hoped."

As I came out of the vision one of the men in the prayer circle looked at me with a big radiant smile and said, "I saw Him too! I watched as He walked into the room from out of the wall in front of you, then He walked over to you and spoke to you!" Although the election did not go the way we prayed, we were all comforted that night by the love and sweetness of God. There were only two choices for people to vote for. I'm convinced that God's choice was not selected.

My voting criteria is always based on three simple principles—pro-life, pro-Israel, and a candidate who supports biblical marriage values that uphold marriage between one man and one woman. Because a leader was selected who was pro-abortion, anti-Israel, and who strongly embraced the homosexual agenda, the newly elected government administration that he assembled made huge strides in tearing down traditional marriage morals between a man and a woman, and a new level of perversion was ushered in like never seen before in America. As you know, he was eventually reelected for a second term, culminating in his "achievements" being celebrated before the world by having the White House lit up at night in symbolic rainbow colors representing their full endorsement of homosexual marriage. The Vice President of the same administration (a self-proclaimed practicing Catholic) contributed to the Westernized effort of redefining the teachings of the Bible by officiating his first marriage—not between a man and a woman but between two men—at the Vice President's official residence, the Naval Observatory. If the other presidential candidates had been elected as President in 2008 or 2012, such a godless agenda would not have gained nearly as much traction and a growing climate of hostility that now exists against Christianity would have been checked.

God doesn't always get what He wants even when His will is clearly expressed. This is due to man's sovereignty and his ability to obey or willfully disobey the will of God. Our prayers can greatly affect this, but they may not always be answered the way we wish because they are dealing with the lives of other people and not our own personal issues where we have control over the outcome. With our own lives we can be much more consistent in attaining answered prayers because we can cooperate with God and do our part to please the Lord through obedience to His Word and asking in accordance with His will.

I think we should also consider factors in prayer that we may not always be aware of, but God knows and He can alter outcomes because of His love and care for us. When growing up as a young child in rural Mississippi, our family did not have any luxuries. We lived out in the wildwood on a small farm and were bused in to school each day along with the other local children. While in the third grade I experienced an unusual occurrence that occurred daily for quite some time while riding the bus home from school. Our bus driver was in his early twenties and he drove with a heavy foot on the gas pedal. We had very few paved roads in the county so the dirt and gravel roads provided ample opportunities for our driver to practice his unorthodox driving skills.

He would drive recklessly, swinging the bus around corners, which caused the bus to fishtail wildly. He would burn out when taking off, and when stopping he would lock down the brakes for 100-foot-long slides on the backwoods roads. Today's professional drift drivers who garner millions of views on YouTube had nothing on this guy. He was doing that stuff decades before it became famous through being filmed with Go-Pro cameras and streamed on the Internet in 4K clarity. As dangerous and foolish as it was (he eventually got fired when I told my third grade teacher, Mrs. Starks), he did have a nice spot in his heart by daily making an unauthorized stop at a small general store to buy gum and candy for himself. This allowed me and all the kids on the bus to get off and go inside a store (without our parents' knowledge) and look at all the candy that we never had access to.

I always wanted to be able to buy a piece of candy, but I didn't even have a nickel to buy one gumball. My brothers and I were poor, like almost everyone else on the bus. But there was one kid whose initials were MM (I called him M&M) who rode the bus who was in fifth grade and he always had an extra dollar to be able to purchase an ample amount of candy for himself. Once, after getting onto the bus after our convenient store stop, he began to open up his bag of candy and slowly eat it. I was sitting on the aisle across from him and was two seats back. I observed closely as he leisurely unwrapped each piece of candy and ate it with great pleasure. Sitting there watching him made me inwardly wish I too could have a piece of candy. Then, M&M turned around slowly and looked at me and with his Southern drawl said, "I don't know why you're ah lookin', cause you sho' ain't gonna get none." Sometimes kids can be so mean to each other.

I never did get any candy. I even prayed and asked God for candy, but still never got any. Two years later I was getting off the bus, and as I walked down the aisle toward the exit door I happened to see that M&M had fallen asleep in his seat. His mouth was wide open as he slept, and I could look right down and see inside of it. As I stared in I was jolted to see that all of his teeth were rotted out! The only thing left where his teeth used to be were black stubs that were recessed below the gumline. In his mouth was a half-melted piece of Starburst candy slowly dissolving away and filling his mouth with sugar even as he slept. The realization hit me that what happened to M&M would have been my same tragedy if I was allowed to eat candy the way I wanted to. I thanked the Lord that He didn't answer my prayer about candy.

In light of this, we should endeavor to always aim for the center of God's will when we pray and be careful with requests for sweet and sugary things. I know that the blessings of God can be seen as sweet, but too much sweet is not good, just as too much sugar in your coffee will make your coffee undrinkable. If some Christians had their way then they would be at the spa every day for six hours getting massages, being fed strawberries dipped in chocolate, eating lavish buffets, engaged in non-stop shopping, and sliding into the valley of decadence that engulfs their carnal passions and desires. We all can enjoy nice things, but we must balance the sweetness with work, prayer, and the joy of overcoming obstacles and difficulties in life. As you pray, strive to avoid areas of uncertainty or vagueness in which you are unsure of what the mind of God is on those issues. Follow the key rule of the heavenly gamebook of prayer by always asking "according to His will." It doesn't matter how seemingly impossible your requests may appear. Impossibilities are not the determining factor. It is the ascertaining of the will of God that is paramount. Pray strong. Pray often. Pray in faith. But always pray inbound, and you will find rich fulfillment in answered prayers.

Chapter Nine

TONGUES AND PRAYING IN THE SPIRIT TO BUILD UP FAITH

In order to bring God's promises into manifestation in our lives, we must be willing to invest time in prayer to see the culmination of our dreams and hopes. Praying in the Spirit can be identified as praying in tongues, as well as praying in our natural language when our hearts are in tune with God's will. To further escalate our effectiveness in prayer, we can use our mind to visualize the desire that God has placed within us and prophetically see it coming to pass. This is very effective particularly when praying in tongues.

Praying in tongues for extended periods of time is a wise investment you can reap the benefits of now as well as sowing into your future. As you pray now, you are bringing the blessings and provision from heaven into the present time. Your faith takes them off of the heavenly supply shelf and deposits them into your current life experience. Faith believes that it has received the promise before it is ever seen. Here is the key of godly visualization while speaking and praying in tongues—you must visualize yourself possessing the promise of God.

For example, as you pray in tongues, if you are sick you need to see yourself in your godly imagination as being healed. What would you do if you were not sick? Where would you go that you cannot go now because of the hindrance caused by the illness? Begin to see yourself now doing the same things you would do as if you were well—taking long walks, going out and enjoying a nice meal, exercising, or planning a vacation. Even if your body cannot currently do these things, you can still "go there" with your mind. Visualize yourself healed and in sound physical condition. Visualize this while you pray in tongues, and your faith for this particular need will rise over time to the point where your heart is able to grab the promise with no strain. The anointing of God containing His healing power will be released through your faith, and then your body naturally responds to the will of God, which is health and wholeness.

As you pray in tongues, paint a visual picture of yourself as being prosperous and abundantly supplied with a financial overflow that empowers you to generously support the work of God. If you visualize yourself as being poor and always struggling, then your expectancy level will be wired to correspond with your thought patterns. When this happens you will expect there to be shortage and insufficiency in your life. We usually receive what we expect, so we need to always be expecting God's best. We must carry an abundant mind-set.

Not everyone in this world is struggling. There are those who live without feeling the heat even while others sit under the sun of searing financial strain. Even though the world's financial system is fragile and is susceptible to volatile swings due to its fear-driven nature, the world is still full of wealth. In America, there are more than ten million Americans with a net worth of at least $1 million. There are about nine million other Americans who are multimillionaires with a net worth of up to $5 million. There are over one million households that are classified as high net worth, having between $5 million and $25 million. There are 540 billionaires in the United States This is just a small national perspective of individual wealth and doesn't include the global picture where we see China and India's developing economies churning out hundreds of new millionaires every single day. There are now over 11,000 Chinese citizens with assets over $30 million. Other countries are prospering as well, enabling many to cross the millionaire threshold for the first time. As of the writing of this book, there are currently 1,810 billionaires in the world. Global wealth is increasing; it's not going backward like some Christians envision. Clearly we see that not everyone is experiencing financial turmoil. This amassing of global wealth is an indicator of multiple end-time Scriptures that reveal that there will be a supernatural transfer of assets of financial resources into the body of Christ. This has happened before among the people of God as demonstrated in the following verse.

He also brought them out with silver and gold, and there was none feeble among His tribes (Psalm 105:37).

For some Christians the above verse seems almost incomprehensible—that three million Israelites coming out of Egypt were all healthy and were recipients of miraculous wealth. God did it once and He's going to do it again. Actually, it's already started happening to those who are walking in the forerunner anointing of miracle wealth that is based on a financial covenant with God. You must decide within your heart that you want to participate in this remarkable moving of the Spirit. This marvelous working of God is just as genuine as a healing movement, any revival, or any outpouring of God's Spirit. It is pure and holy and is sanctioned by Jesus Christ Himself, the Head of the eternal church. Therefore, it is very important that we choose daily to visualize our success lest we lose hope and become engulfed with mental images of financial ruin, job layoffs, or recession. The news on television takes great efforts to report any dismal financial story. The whole time they are broadcasting these gloomy headlines, they (the news personalities) are making generous six-figure incomes (some prime time news anchors are making multi-milliondollar incomes), driving nice vehicles, living in beautiful homes, and broadcasting with three or more cameras that cost $250,000 each. As they announce data about the rise of inflation, the high unemployment rate, and the fragile economy, you can't help but notice that the men newscasters wear a new tailored suit and matching tie every night, and the women newscasters have on a new custom-made designer outfit for every show.

If things are as bad as news reporters say, then why are the news companies so profitable, making literally billions of dollars and operating as global media empires? Most of their content is political spin, media propaganda, and irrelevant information that does not directly impact your life. In other words, they are not broadcasting news with a deep desire to disclose information to you, they are broadcasting news to make money. In today's modern world, that's their entire purpose for doing what they do, and the more sensational and scandalous the headlines are, then the more lucrative are the revenues generated through commercial advertisement that ends up in their pockets. I enjoy watching the news a little in order to get a quick perspective of national and world events. But I like God's news far better. Most of the world's news is negative in content and skewed along political party lines. Even if the content is factually correct it can be toxic to your faith and can make you think the world is falling apart when in reality millions are doing quite well. Guard your inner image of success. This is crucial to making your life move in the right direction. The way you view yourself is the way others will also perceive you. We see this concept reflected in the following verse.

> *There we saw the giants* (the descendants of Anak came from the giants); *and we were like grasshoppers in our own sight, and so we were in their sight* (Numbers 13:33).

If you view yourself as a grasshopper or a person of insignificance, then others will sense your lack of self-worth and you will convince them to look down upon you. View yourself highly as a child of God. See yourself as being unique, irreplaceable, and sought after. Speak good things about yourself and your future. What you believe will sooner or later end up being spoken out of your mouth. Your faith-filled words are the building blocks that are used to construct your future.

> *By faith we understand that the worlds were framed by the word of God, so that the things which are seen were not made of things which are visible* (Hebrews 11:3).

The word for "framed" in the original Greek means to "fit out, mend, repair, remold, reshape, and put in order." It is the same word used in Matthew's gospel where the Scripture says the disciples were *mending* (reshaping and making fit) their nets. The "worlds" (Greek is *aion*) refers to an indefinite period of time. These time periods were shaped and put in order by the "word" (*rhema*) of God. The *rhema* that comes from God is spoken, often as a command. In the proper context of Hebrews, the eleventh chapter, we observe that the entire chapter reveals the potential for a miracle that can take place when a person hears a *rhema* word from God and then acts upon it, continually meditates upon it, and sticks with it until they eventually see the manifestation of the promised word. Apostle Rick Renner is an expert in the language of the Greek New Testament. His paraphrased version of this verse helps to grasp the boundless potential of what can happen when we hear the word of the Lord and act upon it:

> Through faith we understand that different time periods, different decades, centuries, millenniums, different generations within the past history of mankind have been completely altered, remolded, and reshaped by those who received a word from God... (Hebrews 11:3a).[1]

You can alter world history by receiving a word (*rhema*) from God. You will have to visualize the "completed picture" of the *rhema* word before you jump in and begin work. No construction firm builds a skyscraper without first having a blueprint and the required building permits. It requires visualization to diagram and map out all ideas and proposed concepts. We can combine the art of visualization with the dynamic power of praying in the Spirit to unlock necessary revelations to complete important God-given assignments.

> Then God said to Noah, "The end of all flesh has come before Me; for the earth is filled with violence because of them; and behold, I am about to destroy them with the earth. Make for yourself an ark of gopher wood" (Genesis 6:13-14 NASB).

Noah received a *rhema* word from God and thus reshaped the history of world events. That specific event also reshaped the surface of the earth, giving us the Grand Canyon in Arizona and many other global flood-induced natural phenomena. What divine assignment has God placed before you to fulfill? Upon gaining this needed revelation you must then begin to pray it out through the tools of visualization and praying daily in the Holy Spirit. Prophetic fulfillment begins with the initial reception of God's *rhema* word, but we must progress onward from that original point. We must now go to work, just as Noah did through visualization, rendering in your mind's eye the completed project and its various stages. God gave Noah the basic numerical figures to draft a blueprint. Knowing the dimensions allowed Noah to "walk off" the distance and visualize the scope of the overall size of the ship. From that point he could visualize where the stern would be, how far away the bow was, and how much construction space he needed for his new shipyard. Other factors requiring visualization and the need to rely on God in prayer would be exercised with each step of doing something that had never been done before.

For example, God told Noah to "Make for yourself an ark of gopher wood" (Gen. 6:14). Perhaps Noah was unfamiliar with gopher wood. Noah had received a direct word from God but a lot of the fine points were yet to be ironed out. Noah was going to have to use his faith and pray in order to move the project forward. Noah was most likely inexperienced in shipbuilding. Even if he had built a boat before, he had never touched upon a project of this magnitude. Therefore, he probably had a lot of initial questions that he needed accurate answers for. "What species of tree is gopher wood?" "Where can I find gopher wood, because I'm going to need a lot of it?' Perhaps he prayed and went on the Internet to do a Google search about this strange wood. He would then have been surprised to find out that gopher wood is not a certain *type* of wood but a certain *application* of wood. It's amazing what you can learn on the Internet. Of course, I'm joking about Noah using the Internet. We all know the Internet wasn't invented until much later in the days of King David ☺ (another joke).

In 1977, a scientific survey was carried out on an object suggested to be Noah's ark in Turkey near the border of Iran. The large, ship-like object is the length of a football field and rests in a mountainous region at an elevation of 6,300 feet. The results of the experiments carried out upon this object convinced many people that this was the legendary Noah's ark. Some still have doubts whether it is the actual ark, but nevertheless there are still some interesting facts that were discovered in the on-site research of this ancient site.

One of the most intriguing finds was a piece of petrified wood. When this was first found it appeared to be a large beam. But upon closer examination it is actually three pieces of plank that have been laminated together with some kind of organic glue. The bond of the glue was discovered to be harder than the wood itself. The glue was most likely the product of a sticky tree resin or tree bark that had been stewed in a large cauldron and then carefully boiled down. Layers of wooden planks would be coated with this ancient superglue, sandwiched together, and then firmly clamped in place for three or four days. Heat would then somehow be applied during the bonding process, thus making the overall strength of the wood incredible. This is the same technology used in modern plywood. Lamination makes the total strength of the wood many times greater than the combined strength of the pieces. This knowledge was used 6,000 years ago in the ancient world. We can be certain that Noah built the ark skillfully, thoughtfully, and prayerfully according to God's plan and also according to unfolding revelation that he received throughout the build process.

Along with forming proper mental images through visualizing in the Spirit, we have an extra tool that Noah and his sons didn't have in their construction tool chest. Praying in the Spirit, also known as praying in tongues, is unique to the New Testament church and can be used to access the very mind of God. I truly believe that the genius nature of God can be tapped into by the Christian who prays in tongues often. It was the mathematician Mark Kac who said that there are two types of geniuses. First, there is the "ordinary" genius who makes you feel that you could possibly do what they do if only you were one hundred times smarter. Second are those super-rare individuals known as "magical" geniuses. These are the ones whose minds are so phenomenal that what they do is considered to be incomprehensible to the "normal" everyday person. It is often the magical geniuses who are obsessed with mathematical equations that deal with infinity, string theory, black hole physics, and quantum mechanics. They have a hunger to understand the universe and other dimensions. What they are endeavoring to access is the realm of the Spirit, which is granted to the Christian when the Holy Spirit is in manifestation.

Once I spoke in Ohio in a church conference and I felt led of the Spirit to share about some of my experiences with the Lord Jesus in the heavenly realms. After speaking, a gentleman and his wife came up to speak to me. She was a physicist and he was an astrophysicist. The husband said, "Steven, that was an incredible message. This is the type of teaching we scientists need to be hearing. You are sharing with us the very secrets of the universe and you reveal how physics agrees with the Bible through your teaching and stories." I thought I had only preached a basic message, but he and his wife expressed that to them it was one of the most profound teachings they had ever heard. I have no doubt that there is some magical genius potential within all of us because we are made in the image of God.

By the grace of God, I have been able to touch the level of magical genius when under the anointing of the Spirit. Usually it happens without me even knowing it. It's good when I don't know because it keeps me humble and it identifies the true source of the genius, which is God and certainly not me. It all comes from God because all origins of genius are found within the mind of God. In another large conference meeting in which I was ministering, a tremendous anointing began to manifest through me. I simply ministered, and then when the anointing started to lift I concluded my service. A few weeks later, a mature minister of the gospel saw me and he came over to talk to me while I was at a coffee house. He relayed to me how he thought that the former meeting that I ministered in was one of the most awesome meetings he had ever been in. He said the glory emanating from me as I spoke seemed to be so marvelous that I appeared to be as someone speaking from another world. He and the others present in that service said they were simply in awe of how God was flowing through me. From my perspective, the whole time I had ministered in that meeting I thought it was just another "good" meeting. I was completely unaware of how God was falling so heavily upon His people with His mighty presence and the way in which I was engulfed in His glory. Often God will veil His mighty working to the minister so that He gets all the glory.

A few years ago a woman apostle who lives in Long Beach, California, traveled to the South Pacific Islands to minister the gospel. She preached the Word of God to the people, and then afterward gave opportunity for the sick to be healed through the ministry of the laying on of hands. She went down a long line of people, praying for them one by one. Eventually she came to a particular woman in the line. The woman of God was graciously moved by the Spirit to speak to the woman in the prayer line and say, "Stick out your tongue." For some reason or another the woman in line did not stick out her tongue. The minister became divinely agitated at the woman's refusal to obey a simple instruction. So she shouted with great authority and said, "I told you to stick out your tongue!"

Immediately, the woman stuck out her tongue. The audience gasped. Shock went throughout the congregation that was watching. The apostle didn't know why the people were so amazed about the action of a woman sticking out her tongue, so she continued on down the prayer line, praying for the sick. It wasn't until after the meeting concluded that she was informed that the woman who stuck out her tongue had no tongue! From birth the woman was tongueless, but she received a miracle and God gave her a new tongue, even though the servant of God who was ministering was unaware of the high level of glory she was operating in. The magical genius of God flowing through His people is breathtaking to behold. As you visualize and pray for extended periods in tongues *you* will begin to tap into this realm, and God will transport your mind into realms of thought you have never explored before. These are spiritual journeys that you can take with God every day. This will awaken and release the genius within you.

When staring at a blank art canvas, an artist creates an original work according to an image he sees from within his mind or through an outward inspiration taken from a mountain, river, or perhaps something abstract. Once the image is strongly perceived by the artist (visualization), he then begins to paint and bring forth his inspiration. This is what we are doing as we pray in the Spirit while visualizing the intended desire. Out of these times of prayer will come the reality which we have hoped for, a reality that can be seen, touched, and felt. The rewards are worth the time and commitment necessary to experience this. Everything that I am now experiencing in life is because I took the time years ago to go away and pray in tongues for long periods of time. As I did so, I would visualize myself doing certain things. While praying in tongues an inner image would begin to form in my mind and I could see myself within that mental picture acting out certain events. Today, I am doing those very things that once seemed like far-fetched dreams.

For instance, before I ever traveled in ministry to other countries I knew in my heart that it was in the plan of God for my life. Every weekend I would go to a baseball park near my house and pray there for several hours when there was no one there. I would walk back and forth on the bleachers, praying in tongues while visualizing myself traveling to far away countries and preaching the gospel there. At that point it seemed like only a distant dream. I had not a single overseas ministry invitation, and my passport had never been used. But I sowed in prayer and now I'm reaping the harvest of those two specific years in which I spent hours of steady prayer in tongues walking the bleachers. My first international ministry trip was to Uganda in East Africa. The Lord was so kind that He even allowed Kelly and me to be upgraded to first class on our flight from Los Angeles over to Uganda on British Airways. When we landed on the runway of Entebbe Airport in Uganda, Kelly began to cry. Ever since she was a little child growing up in Buena Park, California, she knew that one day she would go to Africa, and now, years after treasuring and developing the image within her heart, she was touching down in the heart of Africa to minister the gospel with me. Since that first international trip, we have flown all over the planet, and we continue to do so today as we visualize our goal of traveling to over one hundred nations in our efforts to preach the gospel.

Even though I had never ministered overseas when starting off in ministry, I still received consistent prophecies that I would be sent by the Lord to the nations. However, I didn't just rest in the prophecy, but I pursued the prophetic word with fervor and passion. When you receive a strong prophetic word from the Lord, what are you going to do with it? Most Christians rejoice over the prophetic word, fully knowing that it is accurate, but why do so many believers fail to receive the manifestation of that prophecy? I believe the reason why is because of a failure of praying in tongues and prophetic visualization. Within every generation God is still speaking and releasing high priority *rhema* words. Take those words and flesh them out by putting meat to the bones. Unwrap the word, examine the word, visualize how you will fulfill the word, pray in the Spirit so that the prophecy or *rhema* word becomes knitted to your heart and calling. See yourself doing the impossible. Remove mental limitations and all excuses for why it can't be done. Break new barriers and do something new and fresh. We are a continuation of the eleventh chapter of Hebrews, living in the eleventh hour, and doing remarkable exploits based on what God has spoken to us to do.

When you receive a word from the Lord, you should prayerfully contend for the fulfillment of that specific word. Pray in tongues and visualize that word coming to pass. Visualization works exceptionally well when you pray in tongues because your mind can relax and focus on a mental picture of the fulfillment of the prophecy. Your mind doesn't understand what your spirit is praying in tongues, so it is free to visualize. This spiritual exercise will usher you into a new level of faith and understanding the marvelous workings of God. No longer will a key prophecy or direct *rhema* word flounder in your life. God's plan for your life will unfold beautifully in all its glory, and it's going to make you so happy as you see it happening before your eyes. Be willing to make the spiritual investment necessary to reap the rewards that God has destined for you.

NOTE

1. Rick Renner, "Bulldog Faith," Cfaith, accessed September 11, 2016, http://www.cfaith.com/index.php/blog/19-articles/faith/15414-bulldog-faith.

Chapter Ten

YOUR FIRST AND YOUR SECOND SLEEP

Earlier in Chapter Five we discovered the symbolism of the nighthawk and saw how we can gain access into the night school of the Spirit. As we exercise our faith to draw near to God and appropriate the blessings of God, we can learn to further utilize our time to a capacious extent. Again, much of this can be carried out at night. King David was well aware of this.

At midnight I will rise to give thanks to You, because of Your righteous judgments (Psalm 119:62).

Because this psalm is an acrostic, there is a tradition that King David used it to teach his young son Solomon the Hebrew alphabet—not just the alphabet for writing letters, but more importantly the alphabet of the spiritual life. There's a lot you can learn at midnight to advance your spiritual life that can be missed during the business of the day. Rising at midnight may sound like an ascetic practice, but it is not so strange when we dig into the history of human sleep behavior. In our modern world in which we live, we are accustomed to viewing a normal sleep cycle as being a block of time usually somewhere around eight hours. In other words, a person would go to bed at 10:00 P.M.

and then wake up at 6:00 A.M. But it appears that when we study this sleep cycle we begin to see that this is a new phenomenon that only dates back to the 1920s. Historian Roger Ekirch is a professor of history at Virginia Tech University. His writings on the subject of sleep, based on sixteen years of study, have pioneered new understanding in the way our former ancestors slept. This knowledge is helping many to reclaim healthier sleeping habits and thus enjoying a better quality of life.

In this chapter I would like to share some insights that I trust you will find helpful in understanding how to find *lost* time that can be used at night for prayer, Scripture meditation, and seeking God.

For thousands of years in the past, mankind has always slept twice each night. They would go to bed when it became dark. In the summer that may be as late as 9:00 P.M. In the winter the night comes much earlier, sometimes around 5:30 P.M. Either way, they would always go to bed when it became dark. For instance, in the fall season they would go to bed at 7:00 P.M. Then they would sleep for five hours and naturally wake up at midnight. After staying awake for an hour or two they would then go back to sleep for another two or three hours. Their sleep consisted of sleeping twice each night in two shorter periods. This was the standard way of sleeping back then. The interesting case with children, however, is different. When children go to bed, they naturally sleep all the way through until daybreak. They sleep comfortably in one long segment of eight or nine hours. This gives today's parents a remarkable opportunity to have some "me time" at midnight that perhaps they didn't think was available.

Why are our sleep patterns so different today than the classic historical example? They are different because of *electricity*. Before Thomas Edison invented the light bulb, people would fall asleep after sunset. Street lighting, indoor lighting, computers, smartphones, tablets, and other light-emitting electronic devices now exist that were unknown in previous generations. These devices disrupt the natural release of the hormone melatonin, which helps regulate sleep and wake cycles (the circadian clock). God designed your body with a built-in biological clock. Melatonin production in the body is triggered by darkness. When we watch television or read on our tablets before going to bed, we block melatonin and thus interfere with our body's chemical clock.

Dr. Thomas Wehr is considered to be the world's leading sleep researcher. As a professional psychiatrist he was curious as to what would happen if he put average Americans into an environment where all artificial lights are removed at sunset. He and his assistants at the National Institute of Mental Health recruited 15 healthy adult male volunteers. They went about their normal activities during the day, then went to an assigned sleep lab in the early evening. "We had our subjects go into the dark at 6 P.M., lie down and rest," Wehr says. The lights were turned back on at 8:00 the next morning, which simulated a long, fourteen-hour winter night. At first the subjects slept an average of eleven hours a night. But after a month they all settled into a very distinct sleeping pattern. The sleep study found that they slept in two sessions of concentrated sleep that also included a wakeful period in the middle, lasting a few hours. The study was published in 1993 in the *American Journal of Physiology*. "You might think that lying awake for two hours would be a kind of torture," Wehr says. "But it wasn't at all." This awake period of time is known as *quiet wakefulness*. It is a time when we are blissfully flushed with prolactin, and our *night brains* allow highly creative thoughts to emerge and interweave as they would in a dream condition.

Jessa Gamble is an award-winning writer from Oxford, England. Concerning the effects of the first and second sleep, combined with a short nap during the day, she says, "There is a surge of prolactin the likes of which a modern day (person) never sees," she says that those who retrain their bodies to experience segmented sleep end up "feeling so awake during the daytime that they realize they're experiencing true wakefulness for the first time in their lives." Prolactin is a naturally occurring hormone in men and women that is released through a healthy sleep rhythm. Prolactin causes us to feel peaceful and calm. It is even released in chickens, which allows a hen to sit calmly on an egg all day long. The original sleep cycle provided a means for us to be super productive and sharp during the day. It also provided a great framework for an atmosphere conducive to a peaceful haven of prayer at midnight. A strong prayer life is based on calmness, quietness, and an inner peace that enables us to sit still without fidgeting and squirming.

At midnight I will rise (Psalm 119:62).

David was able to rise at midnight in a wide-awake condition in which he could pray in serenity, quietly meditate, and compose thought-provoking music under the inspiration of the Holy Spirit. When we look at the Jewish history of sleep, we begin to recognize the original pattern of dual stages of sleep and the lasting effect it had upon the Jewish prayer life. In the latter part of the 1500s, Rabbi Isaac Luria instituted what became known to the Jews as Tikkun Hatzot, which is a Jewish ritual prayer recited each night after midnight as an expression of mourning and lamentation over the destruction of the Temple in Jerusalem. Rabbi Luria was a Jewish mystic who lived in Safed, Israel, which is in the region of Galilee. He is considered the father of Kabbalah, which is a form of Jewish mysticism that endeavors to explain the Scriptures from an esoteric perspective.

We should not find it surprising that midnight prayers would be initiated by mystics. A mystic is someone who is not satisfied with normal dosages of spirituality but has a much greater craving for devotion and prayer. King David was a prophet and mystic. Rabbi Luria was a mystic who saw the literal meaning of the Scripture but also looked for spiritual applications of the sacred text. Actually, all world religions have within their followers a small group that can be identified as mystics. Among the Muslims you have the Sufis. The Hindu religion has the gurus, swamis, and yogis. Among the Buddhist monks you have those who practice samadhi, which is an extreme form of meditation. Within Christianity we see the Roman Catholic Church, where we have the recognized saints who displayed almost unfathomable levels of devotion to Christ through fasting, mortification, penance, and prayers.

Among the evangelical Christians, the Christian mystic is not so well celebrated or understood. That's OK because God has created a healthy balance within the body of Christ. The evangelicals are responsible for carrying the practicality of the gospel. If you live in the desert or in a hidden cave on the side of a mountain and pray all day and night, then nobody is going to print or publish any Bibles, no television networks would be launched, Christian hospitals would not be built, nor would the gospel be spread through numerous Bible translations, nor would overseas missionary work be carried out. It's a brilliant balance when you can combine the right amount of spirituality together with the practicality of getting things done. We all need the dual qualities of spiritual devotion and knowing when to complete work assignments.

The enduring legacy of the Christian mystic within the church is the thin red line that can be traced all the way through from the early apostles to the Desert Fathers who wandered in the Judean wilderness and even up to the present day. You may be wondering, "How do I find a Christian mystic? Do they still exist today?" Yes, they are still around, and they still pray at midnight. You have to be careful if you start praying at midnight or else that anointing may just rub off on you as well. But that wouldn't be too bad would it—to become a mystic and be in the same category as King David, John the Baptist, Francis of Assisi, John the Beloved, Teresa of Avila, Joseph of Cupertino, Sadhu Sundar Singh, Padre Pio, and the numerous other great saints?

We have to ask ourselves, "Why did Rabbi Luria lay out guidelines for midnight prayer?" He did this because he was disturbed at how the Jews were using their time in between their two sleep cycles to do things that were not of a spiritual nature. For instance, many of the Jews would wake up at midnight and go outside of their homes and smoke tobacco. Others would carry on conversation with their neighbors. Many snacked at this time, while other married Jews enjoyed sexual relations with their spouse. Rabbi Luria wanted the Jewish community to grasp that even though Europe was slowly moving toward a new age of science and industry there was still a great need to have a quality spiritual life. He taught that the glory of the Messiah would express itself in the physical world in 1948 on a Friday. Over 400 years later, Israel was officially recognized as a sovereign State in 1948 and it was ratified by the United Nations on a Friday. Rabbi Luria hoped his prayer guidelines would stir the men to pray at night so that they could discern the times and seasons of God, as well as the panoramic plan of God for humanity.

After the expulsion of all the Jews from Spain in 1492, many of the 100,000 displaced Jews and leading rabbis moved to Safed. Even though Safed was ruled by the Muslim leader Suleiman I and then by Selim I, the city of Safed still became a global center for Jewish learning as well as a nucleus of lucrative regional trading. In the year of 1584, there were 32 synagogues registered in the town. Rabbi Luria's desire for the Jews to have a prayer guideline at midnight produced over time many scholars of the Scriptures as well as helping to inspire many Orthodox Jews for hundreds of years along with those today who still pray the Tikkun Hatzot weekly, and some even pray it daily.

The practice of praying at midnight also finds its place within certain Christian monastic groups. A dear friend of mine who is a Roman Catholic priest received much of his religious training while he was a Benedictine monk for nine years. The monks follow what is known as the *Rules of Saint Benedict*, written around the year of 530, and one of the instructions calls for an hour of prayer from midnight to 1:00 A.M. Prayers have been ascending to heaven every night at midnight through these devoted men for almost five hundred years. The Eastern Orthodox churches as well as some Anglican churches also have midnight prayer services. But it is always the Word of God that serves as the true pacesetter for all spiritual inspiration. We see in the Scripture that God's people have been active in their faith at the midnight hour throughout the generations.

> *But Samson stayed in bed until midnight when he got up, took hold of the doors of the city gate along with the two gateposts, and pulled them out, bar and all. He put them on his shoulders and took them to the top of the mountain overlooking Hebron* (Judges 16:3 HCSB).

Samson had the midnight urge to go to the gym and do a weight workout. The 24-hour fitness concept had not yet gained traction, so he decided to pursue a different option. He arose at midnight, most likely after the first sleep. His weight lifting needs were met through pulling the massive doors of the city gate completely apart. That offered him a good back and lower leg workout. Realizing the need to also include a good cardio routine in order to stay lean, he then proceeded to carry the gates 38 miles away and uphill with an increase in altitude of 3,200 feet, where he then dropped them in a triumphant display of spiritual power and sweat equity. The 21,400-pound gates were shattered at midnight. The Holy Spirit can remove and demolish every barrier, hindrance, obstacle, and gate that stands before you if you will only get up and pray.

> *Gideon and his 100 men came to the edge of the camp. It was the beginning of the midnight watch just at the change of the guards. They blew their rams' horns and smashed the jars they were holding in their hands* (Judges 7:19 GW).

Some Bible teachers have said that the middle watch was from 10:00 P.M. until 2:00 A.M. However, it appears that the ancient Jews had only three night watches, whereas Jews living in the time of Jesus had four night watches due to the Roman military method of dividing up night segments. In Gideon's case, the night invasion would have unfolded just after midnight on the 12:00 to 4:00 shift. Keep in mind that they didn't have clocks back then, so the event couldn't be timed to an exact minute, but this appears to be another midnight event.

> *Now it happened at midnight that the man was startled, and turned himself; and there, a woman was lying at his feet. And he said, "Who are you?" So she answered, "I am Ruth, your maidservant. Take your maidservant under your wing, for you are a close relative"* (Ruth 3:8-9).

Redemption for Ruth began to unfold at midnight. Perhaps Boaz was waking up from his first sleep when he encountered Ruth lying there. The Holy Spirit can work at night just as easily as He can during the day.

> *But at midnight Paul and Silas were praying and singing hymns to God, and the prisoners were listening to them* (Acts 16:25).

You would think Paul and Silas would be asleep from exhaustion after having been beaten with rods. If they can arise to pray at midnight after a tremendous beating, then how much more can we arise after lying in a comfortable bed with a fluffy pillow?

It appears the awake time in between the two sleep cycles has been a long running practice for the Jews and for other cultures as well. In some ways we have only touched the tip of the iceberg concerning prayers at night. Many rabbis prayed from midnight until 3:00 each night. But this time slot was expanded due to a special drink that eventually made its way into Israel in the late 1570s. The drink was already being enjoyed in Yemen and Egypt, particularly by the Muslim Sufis who discovered that this drink had a marvelous effect of gently pushing away drowsiness. Its bitter taste could be made pleasant by adding sugar and a little cream, and when served almost boiling hot it added to its pleasing nature. The drink was coffee, and once the rabbis realized its potential many of them increased their prayer and study time beyond the already sacrificial time of 12:00 to 3:00 and began to go from midnight until 6:00 in the morning. My practice is to always have a cup of coffee at 3:30 a.m. after crossing beyond my first hour of prayer. It makes the second hour comfortable and it gives me something to look forward to. Keep in mind that what works well for me may not be ideal for you. It's perfectly fine for you to establish your devotional time according to your own needs and desires. It may also take some experimentation for several weeks before you find what time-frame suits you best. Feel free to get up and pray at different times as you search for what is most comfortable and conducive for you. There is no "wrong way" to do this, so have fun in exploring and establishing a dedicated time for prayer in the night.

As an end-time generation, we live in a difficult world where we have many challenges with our schedules due to constant activity. Conflicting early mornings followed by late nights can do a lot to confuse our inner body clocks. Many people suffer from insomnia. Drug and pharmaceutical companies are happy to sell their drugs to help you get to sleep. But I would suggest that if you can't fall asleep you should not take drugs, but pray. If you're lying awake in bed and can't sleep, then why not pray? It certainly wouldn't do any harm. Pray in the dark, and when you get drowsy then you can fall asleep. Through the power of His shed blood the Lord Jesus is able to heal you from insomnia and every other form of sickness. If you suffer from insomnia, trust Him for your healing now. Also do what you can to facilitate healthy sleep habits. Make sure your bedroom is dark and there are no ambient lights to hinder your sleep. You may want to try a small device that emits white noise or pink noise. These gentle and steady sounds block out external noises that often inter-rupt your sleep. Kelly and I always take a small device that produces the pleasant sound of a rotating fan. This works great in drowning out background noise in hotels where people slam doors, talk loud in hallways at all hours of the night, and make noises that can disrupt your sleep.

Over time I have trained myself to pray in the middle of the night. While I would like to go to bed at 8:00 at night, I find it impossible to do so. Normally I go to bed at 10:30 P.M. Because of this I don't nor-mally get up at midnight because if I did then I would only have had one and a half hours of sleep and that would cause me to feel wiped out. It helps when I have four hours of sleep during my first sleep ses-sion. This allows me to get up at 2:30, which is my covenant hour of prayer time. I'll normally pray for two hours. If my morning schedule is not super busy, then I may pray for three or four hours and then go to sleep for two or three hours of rest before starting my day. Once my day gets rolling it's difficult to pray when the sun is up for any type of length because of the many demands that come at me from all direc-tions. As you pray in between the two segments of sleep, I trust you will soon become a lifelong student of the night school of the Spirit. In order to facilitate your entry into this elite school of higher learning and spiritual education, I present to you my *seven royal rules for praying at night.*

SEVEN ROYAL RULES FOR PRAYING AT NIGHT

Rule 1. Set an alarm. Good intentions are not enough. Don't risk oversleeping. If you have to, put the alarm clock out of arm's reach so that you have to get out of bed to turn it off. I have had my personal angel wake me up many times. He will come and grab my wrist and say, "Get up, it's time to pray." When ministering overseas and away from my wife Kelly, often Kelly's personal angel will come and wake me up. Her angel sounds just like Kelly. Their voices are identical. One of the personal guardian angels assigned to Kelly is a female angel and this particular one likes to visit me when I am far away from home. Male angels speak with a male voice. Female angels speak with a female voice. There is no gender confusion in heaven, even though there seems to be much of it in the earth today. But even having had many angelic encounters that assist me with prayer, I still set an alarm every time I sleep to make sure that I get up.

Rule 2. Get out of bed. Don't try praying in bed because you will soon drift back to sleep. "He went out...to a solitary place" (Mark 1:35). Jesus got up and out of bed and *went somewhere* quiet to pray. If you do this, you have won 70 percent of the battle of discomfort. It gets easier once you've done this vital step.

Rule 3. You must not miss your appointed time of prayer. Take it seriously, just as if you were going to a university class, because in many ways you are going to class. If you're not in class, you can't learn. Attendance is mandatory. You should not miss more than three classes per month.

Rule 4. Keep your eyes open. When you follow this simple key you are almost certain to be strong in prayer and become a long-term nighthawk. It may seem strange to keep your eyes open in the dark, but if you close them you will be certain to become drowsy. If you were in a regular class setting in a university, it would displease the teacher to see you sitting in class with your eyes closed. Keep your eyes open throughout the entire prayer session or you risk falling asleep.

Rule 5. Always be on time for your covenant hour of prayer. You are meeting the Lord, and He is meeting you. If your set time is 2:30 A.M., then be sitting on the couch at 2:25. If I wake up at 2:10 I just go ahead and get up and go to the couch and start praying at that time. It never hurts to be early, but it's not polite to be late when someone else is waiting for you.

Rule 6. Do not check e-mails, read the news, or become involved in other *daily* activities. You can do those things later in the day. "He went out and departed to a solitary place; and there *He prayed*." Jesus did not read the Jerusalem Post, New York Times, or check the online weather report. *He prayed*. If you're not sure what to pray then here are a few suggestions.

1   The Lord's Prayer (Matthew 6:9–13)

2.   Paul's prayer to know Christ (Ephesians 1:17–23)

3.   Paul's prayer for strength and to know God's love (Ephesians 3:14–21)

4.   Paul's prayer for spiritual fruitfulness (Philippians 1:9–11)

5.   Paul's prayer to know the will of God (Colossians 1:9–14) (This is my favorite prayer in the Bible.)

6.   Paul's benediction prayer (Hebrews 13:20-21)

7.   Pray the Psalms; there are 150 to choose from.

Rule 7. Make yourself a hot drink. Rabbis have been drinking coffee at night for hundreds of years to help stay awake longer for extended prayer, so we can learn from their example. Kelly drinks a dark and bold coffee roast. I'm the exact opposite; I drink a milder roasted coffee with sugar and extra cream. But as I go into my second hour of prayer that cup of hot coffee sure feels good to hold, to smell the pleasing aroma, and to slowly savor the soothing taste. Before I go to sleep I get my coffee cup ready. I put two small scoops of sugar in it, then I place my Seattle's Best Toasted Hazelnut blend single serving K-Cup into the Keurig machine so that when I wake up I'm quiet as a mouse and I don't disturb others in the house. All I have to do at this point is push a single button, add some cream, and then I'm ready to continue on in prayer.

Jesus prayed in the dark for extended periods of time before the sun ever came up. If you will do the same thing then the promise contained in the following verse will soon begin to blossom in your life as well.

> *Now in the morning, having risen a long while before daylight, He went out and departed to a solitary place; and there He prayed. And Simon and those who were with Him searched for Him. When they found Him, they said to Him, "**Everyone is looking for You**" (Mark 1:35–37).*

The Lord Jesus revealed to me that when His people seek Him at night, then what was said about Him will also be said about you, namely that, "Everyone is looking for you." Your prayer life is the catalyst for mighty anointing and favor. People will search for you. It's as if everyone is looking for you. Why? It's because you become like Jesus. The Spirit comes on you and you carry the answers, the anointing, the word, the hope, and the leadership that they need. So if you practice this spiritual discipline of praying at night, they will come looking for you too!

Chapter Eleven

Stepping Into Jehu's Chariot

With an established format of building your life upon the principles of God's Word, united with a powerful prayer life, you are now ready to fully possess the promises of God by using your faith. In order for faith to work properly, it has to be specific. It's similar to shooting with a bow and arrow in that you have to aim at the specified bull's-eye target and not just shoot randomly into the air. The goal is to hit the center of your target. In this chapter I would like to share about targeting your faith for a special vehicle to prophetically connect with the anointing of God's Spirit that rested upon King Jehu, the ancient king of Israel who was used by God to overthrow the wicked Queen Jezebel. King Jehu and his unconventional and irrational methods stand as a witness and an enduring symbolic reference of overcoming in the last days in which we live.

This topic may not be of absolute precedence for some, and that's certainly understandable. Many people in crowded cities have no need of a vehicle. They simply ride the subway train, take a taxi, call an Uber driver, or walk because of the near proximity to work, restaurants, shopping, and church. Because of this, there isn't an enthusiasm in owning a vehicle because there is no direct need for one. In many ways this is a blessing because it allows your life to be simplified, and it's also one less *faith-project* that you have to expend your faith on. This frees you to focus your faith on other areas where it is needed. However, for most people who live outside of congested cities it is pretty much a necessity to have a vehicle to commute to work and back and for other requirements of daily life. So, as long as you need one, why not use your faith for one that you really like?

I would like to ask you the following question. Is a vehicle simply a means to travel from point A to point B in the most economical and utilitarian fashion? Is that all we should expect or hope for in a vehicle—just a basic means to move from one place to another with no perks, comforts, or frills? I believe mundane religious teaching that's packaged through the traditions of men endeavors to make our lives sterile and boring. Yet God created us with emotions, and there are certain things that catch our interest—one of them being automobiles.

Henry Ford is famous for having developed and mass produced the first car in 1908, which was called the Ford Model T. It sold for only 240 dollars. Since then, the automotive industry has expanded in its ability to provide drivers with choices and features that are almost unlimited in scope. In the early days, cars were offered in just a few basic colors such as black, red, or green. Now cars can be custom ordered in any color, even metallic or neon colors. Options are endless from the choice of horsepower, manual or automatic transmission, interior fabrics, even down to the rims and tires, all of which can be greatly customized. It seems Americans especially have always had a special love interest with cars.

For ten years I lived in Moravian Falls, which is in Wilkes County in North Carolina. NASCAR originated out of this small county decades ago. For many people in the region, having a fast car was a necessity for social acceptance as well as for bootlegging moonshine. Several years ago when I was pastoring there, I was talking to one of my deacons and his wife on a Sunday after church. They had grown up locally in Wilkes County, and I asked them how they met. With a twinkle in her eye the wife said, "I'll never forget the day I first saw him. I was hanging out with some friends and I heard this guy start up his truck, and the engine sounded so awesome! I saw him in that truck and knew instantly that he was the man I was going to marry." For her, a loud engine, gobs of horsepower, and a sweet man with kind Southern hospitality were enough to seal the deal for a blissful marriage. Some people seem to have the "car bug" in their blood even if they aren't from the country but live in the city. A Ferrari can drive by and almost every guy will turn his head to follow the prancing red pony that looks like art in motion. They have said in American folklore that the way to win a man's heart is through his stomach. This would refer to a wife serving generous portions of good home cookin' to her husband to make him feel pleased and happy. But it could be that the way to a man's heart is not through his stomach, but through his garage. It's not just men who take an interest in vehicles, but women also prefer to drive a safe, clean, reliable, and nice vehicle. One thing's for sure—having a nice car sure beats walking or riding a skateboard, especially when going uphill.

I want to speak to the heart of those who would dare to believe God for a vehicle that brings Him glory and is a constant reminder of His grace to live in victory in all areas of life. This specialized usage of faith may seem to be overdone to some, perhaps too bold for others who prefer to never rock the boat. But one thing I've learned about faith is that the bolder you are with your faith, the better the results you will get. Perhaps there may be a few people who are concerned, maybe even a little edgy, about having something that others perceive to be too nice and which they feel they may have to apologize to others for having. Some believers have been influenced through preaching that supports a scarcity and survivalist mentality. But there are a generous number of Scriptures that release to us the potential to receive beyond what we would even dare to ask God for, as noted in the following verse.

> Now to Him who is able to [carry out His purpose and] do superabundantly more than all that we **dare ask or think [infinitely beyond our greatest prayers, hopes, or dreams]**, according to His power that is at work within us (Ephesians 3:20 AMP).

You have the authorization to ask, even to ask with daring, for a vehicle that makes your heart happy. The above Scripture from the book of Ephesians covers your "dream" vehicle because God is able to do more than what you ask or dream. Another Scripture that speaks to our desires would be the following:

> Delight yourself also in the Lord, and He shall give you the **desires of your heart** (Psalm 37:4).

Our English language has roots in the German language, and we see hints of this in Martin Luther's German translation of Psalm 37:4. For the word *desire* he uses the word *wunsch,* which being translated into English is our word *wish.* God will give you the wishes, the desires, of your heart. What kind of vehicle do you wish for? Be honest with yourself and don't pretend to be super spiritual and say, "That doesn't really matter to me, Pastor Steven, I'm content to simply walk because walking is good exercise." Yes, walking is good exercise, but it's not suitable when your job is thirty miles from home or when you need to take your family to church across town when it's raining or in the cold of winter.

It's so easy for religious defense mechanisms to kick in and suggest that it's not "spiritual" to have a nice vehicle. Actually, your whole life is supposed to be spiritual, every minute of every day, and not just on Sundays when going to church for a few hours. Indoctrination through misguided teaching and fear-of-man mind-sets would suggest that we should all just drive a modest vehicle that doesn't attract attention. But this unscriptural method that wears a garment of false humility doesn't present us with a justifiable explanation regarding the gorgeous peacock and his flamboyant coat of many colors. We should be mindful that the devil did not create the peacock—God did. If God created the peacock with his attention-grabbing iridescent plumage along with another group of outrageously colored birds known as the birds of paradise, then you should feel deeply comfortable driving a nice car, even an exotic car. God is the author of exotic. God's natural creation reflects His style, His glory, and His taste for art and even at times certain eye-popping productions. When you look closely at the beak of a toucan you will see that it appears his bill colors were airbrushed on, with each bird having a different color effect that is marvelous to behold. Let's not forget the exquisite butterflies with their brilliant colored wings as well, which bring us joy when we see them resting on a brightly colored flower God also made. God is the originator of beauty and extravagant customization, so it stands to reason that we should have liberty and creative expression also in what we drive. God's people should lead the way in this category.

God wants you to drive a vehicle that makes you happy. We are made in His image with the same inner desire to enjoy and appreciate nice things. Never lose your passion in life for fun. Refuse to be molded by unscriptural religious traditions into some type of robotic clone so that you end up driving a vehicle you don't even like. You can refuse to bypass normal and put your faith to work for an exceptional vehicle. Stretch for your dream because you can reach what you want with God's help.

Every time you get in your car you should feel blessed and mindful of the goodness of God. Some Christians would feel guilty driving a luxury car because they view it as being excessive to have a nice car.

Oftentimes these same believers think that anything that's nice should be considered excessive and unnecessary. This method of thinking does not agree with the Word of God, nor does it make practical sense when closely examined. The very fact that a person owns a car automatically places them into a lofty position simply because most of the world's population does not own a vehicle. Once I ministered in a certain country where the church that hosted me was very poor. The church had over four hundred members but only one member had a car, and that's because that particular person was a policeman who drove the city's police car to church. So the very fact that you own a car regardless of its condition or shape places you in a category far above "normal" people.

If a sincere but misguided person insists that we should all be normal and non-excessive, then that person should either walk or ride a bicycle everywhere they go because this is still the primary way that billions of people get around today. It's also a fact that 4.2 billion people don't have toilets. Should those of us who have modern plumbing get rid of our toilets, dig a hole in the ground, refuse to use toilet paper, and become like the majority of people, all for the sake of not being "excessive"? To do so would certainly invite the scourge of hookworm back into our nation. It was the wealthy businessman John D. Rockefeller who set out with determination to eradicate hookworm in the early twentieth century in America. Hookworm was a public health threat to those living in poor rural areas within the southern states. It was attributed to people using the bathroom in the bushes and then barefoot people stepping on the parasites that were in the feces. Rockefeller established teaching networks to instruct children to wear shoes and for outhouses to be built. Instructors went door to door teaching the principles of hygiene and also hosted picnics to talk about testing and treatment. Within five years the hookworm epidemic was almost completely wiped out. Prosperity and wealth solve problems. Poverty and scarcity do not carry the empowerment to fix problems but add to the dilemma of human suffering.

The flaw with the train of thought of settling for "status quo" is that from a global perspective status quo is living in lack and poverty. You can't force someone to live at somebody else's standard, nor would you want to when the standard is so low. If we try to please everybody and all function on the lowest common denominator, then we're all going to end up walking or riding on horseback when we should be letting the horses beneath the hoods of modern vehicles transport us in comfort and ease. It is a false humility rooted in the fear of man that hinders many of God's precious people from driving a nice vehicle. Somehow we think that when we get to heaven we will then receive God's best, but while we are down here on earth we are unworthy. Well, if we are unworthy now what makes us think we will be worthy later? Yet, the Scripture reveals that we are qualified now to be blessed, and with a good conscience we can drive a "heart's desire" vehicle through the shed blood of Jesus Christ.

The last vehicle I drove was a true blessing in my life. Even the purchase of my vehicle was blessed by God. When I went to visit a local dealership to consider a purchase I was quickly greeted by an experienced salesman who went with me to walk around the property to show me the vast inventory. They had many models available in the style I was looking at. As you know a certain model can vary greatly in price depending on what options it may have. The salesman began to answer certain questions I had and was showing me the different vehicles that were in my price category. But as we looked at the various vehicles, the dealership's burglar alarm went off and made it impossible to view the vehicles in that area because of the piercing noise. Speaking as loud as he could so that I could hear him over the alarm, the salesman suggested we go to a far lot where there was a vehicle he wanted to show me. The lot was so far away that when we reached it we were out of range of the alarm. I noticed the alarm happened to turn off once he showed me the vehicle he wanted me to see. I truly believe an angel of the Lord caused that alarm to flare up to move me away from what I was willing to settle for, and instead get me to the right location and into a vehicle that I desired and would much rather have.

Upon arriving at the other lot I was greeted by the most amazing truck I had ever seen. It was also the most expensive vehicle on the lot. Examining its rugged exterior and comfortably inviting interior I felt like this would be an awesome truck to own. The salesman explained to me that if I drove this truck then people would be staring due to the bling factor that it possessed. It was a limited edition with special modifications that ensured there would not be anyone else in my zip code, or even the entire county, who had one like mine. I felt the truck would be a suitable witness of the goodness of God in my life. The peace of God was strongly present, so by faith I signed on the dotted line and it was mine. The salesman drove with me to the gas station so that I could receive a complimentary fill-up. When filling up the tank other men who were filling up their vehicles began to walk over to me and ask me, "What kind of truck is that?!"

Everywhere I went the truck was a testimony. This took place nonstop at gas stations where men would walk over to me as I pumped the gas and inquire about my vehicle, wanting to know where I got it and what modifications were done to it. It always gave me an opportunity to share with them that, "The Lord blessed me with my ride." One time a particular man walked over to me at a gas station while I was refueling and he said to me, "That's an awesome truck. I've never seen one of those in this state before. Did you make any modifications on it?"

I replied, "Yes, it's had some special upgrades done to it. The Lord blessed me with this truck."

When I spoke that he walked away with disgust and said, "Great truck, but I don't want anything to do with Jesus!" The vehicle was a witnessing tool for Christ everywhere I went. To some it was the fragrance of Christ, to others the fragrance of death, but either way they received the witness of Jesus through the avenue of a motor vehicle. The monthly payments I made on the truck were the easiest payments I've ever made on any vehicle. Although they were the largest payments I had ever made, I stepped out in faith and not a single payment was a struggle to make, nor was a payment ever late. The payments were technically not in the budget, but God increased my budget to meet the need, and I'm so happy I got what I *wanted* instead of just what I *needed* because with God's blessing it ended up getting paid for in full anyhow.

An anointed apostle of God from Singapore, Dr. Jedidiah Tham, shared with me that he wanted to purchase a vehicle that reflected the nature of his ministry. The name of his ministry is Living Lilies, so after praying about what vehicle to purchase he chose a new Lexus because it has an L emblem on the front and an L emblem on the back, thus symbolically referring to his ministry that has two primary L letters in it. Every time he drives his car he is mindful of his important ministry calling and the work that God has assigned him to do. He has driven me around Singapore in his beautiful, debt-free car while I ministered there.

You know, the devil doesn't mind if you drive a junky old broken down car, but if you try to get something nice he gets all upset and tries to derail you. Be persistent and bold in your faith to acquire a good vehicle that speaks well with your Christian testimony. I believe that God's people should drive the best. I especially believe that God's ministers should drive the best. While speaking with a prophet friend from Canada at an overseas meeting, he told me of a unique car-buying experience he had. After saving his money he went down to a particular dealership and said, "I want to buy the most expensive vehicle on your lot." The salesman was happy to oblige and showed him a beautiful Lincoln Navigator with all the bells and whistles. The prophet bought it on the spot, paid for it, and drove off with it. As he drove off the lot with his new vehicle, he looked back in the rear-view mirror and saw an evil principality standing in the empty space where the vehicle was formerly parked. The evil spirit was frustrated and very irritated that a minister had just bought the best vehicle on the lot. The enemy is powerless against any believer who has trust and confidence in the Word of God.

It's very possible that God could divinely instruct you to purchase an expensive automobile for your personal safety and protection. There was a great prophet of God in India who ministered to millions of people. He lived his life out and has now passed on to heaven, but his powerful ministry continues through the capable leadership of his son today. This prophet shared the deeply moving story of the tragedy that came into his life through disobedience to Jesus of not purchasing a Mercedes Benz. The Holy Spirit moved upon this prophet three distinct times, each time urging him to purchase a Mercedes Benz. The prophet overrode the guidance of the Holy Spirit with the mistaken idea of trying to be frugal and not wanting to be viewed as someone who misused the Lord's funds on an expensive vehicle.

In May 1986, the prophet was driving with his wife and two children when he was involved in a terrible accident in which his seventeen-year-old daughter was killed. The prophet suffered much injury, including the fracture of both hands. In unspeakable sorrow over the loss of his daughter, the prophet poured his heart out to God looking for answers and comfort. Indeed, the Lord did bring supernatural comfort to His servant and raised him up to once again minister effectively to the multitudes. The Lord also lovingly informed this dear saint that He had tried multiple times to lead him to a buy Mercedes Benz because the enemy was plotting to take him out through a vehicle accident. A Mercedes Benz has an incredibly strong frame that surrounds its passengers offering a very high level of safety. When God gives us a "word of wisdom," it is imperative that we obey. A word of wisdom is a supernatural revelation by the Spirit of God concerning the divine purposes and plans of God. The word of wisdom will always speak toward your future and what is in front of you. When a word of wisdom is obeyed it brings tremendous blessing. But if it is disobeyed then the results can be harmful, even disastrous to us, and sometimes to others around us.

I was flying into a particular nation to record television programs at the studio of a highly respected prophet. Upon my arrival I was picked up in a beautiful white Mercedes Benz, which offered a comfortable ride to the hotel and studio. The car was brand new, and my prophet friend explained to me how he acquired this wonderful vehicle for the Lord's work. He informed me that recently while in prayer the Lord spoke to him to purchase a new Mercedes Benz. My friend is very accountable with ministry finances and lives a very low-key lifestyle, so he endeavored to ignore what the Lord told him. Then one day the Lord spoke to him very clearly and said, "You are making the same mistake that _____ (He mentioned the former prophet by name) made." Upon hearing this my friend was struck with determination to obey the Lord. Without having the financial resources to acquire a new Mercedes, he inquired of the Lord what he should do. The Lord responded and said, "Ask your ministry partner, Mr. _____ (a local businessman) to give you the money for the new car."

My friend explained to me that he felt so embarrassed to do this because he thought, "What if my ministry partner thinks I'm just using him for his money? Especially money to buy a luxury car with?" So, because of his reluctance he changed his request and asked the specific ministry partner if he could instead "borrow" $100,000 for a new Mercedes Benz for the ministry. The businessman said that he and his wife would take a few days to pray about it and then get back to him with a response.

After a few days of prayer, the businessman contacted my friend and said, "The Lord told me *not* to lend you the $100,000 for the car. He said I am not to lend you the money, but rather I am to *give* it to you freely as an offering." With the money in hand my prophet friend then went and purchased the new Mercedes. Almost immediately after that, the businessman who gave the offering received a construction contract that profited him exactly $100,000. A word from God should always be obeyed, even if it means to purchase a certain vehicle. This particular country where this minister lives has very lax traffic regulations, which are not easily monitored or enforced by the law. Out of the many countries I have visited over the years, I have never been to any other country that even comes close to matching the zaniness of the driving styles as in this country. It's not unusual to see three, four, or even five people riding on one motorcycle all at the same time, with no one wearing a helmet, while driving at freeway speeds. God is concerned about your safety and your well-being. This doesn't mean you need to drive a tank, but it simply means that you should travel in modern standards of safety. We don't want to give the devil any open door to access our lives through an unsafe environment.

Jesus said, "According to your faith let it be to you" (Matt. 9:29). What type of vehicle do you have faith for? Your desire must correspond with your level of faith. You can't go beyond your current measure of faith. If the greatest amount of weight you can bench press is 250 pounds, then you cannot realistically expect to put 600 pounds on the bar and press it. To attempt to do so is only going to lead to failure and quite possibly a severe injury. You need to know what you can lift with your faith. Your faith level is the place where you feel comfortable. You're not aiming too low, but you also aren't aiming beyond what you believe in your heart God will do for you at the current season in your life. If your faith level is at the Toyota stage, then it's not time to be shopping for a Rolls Royce. Eventually, you can reach higher levels; oftentimes we move forward in a way that's similar to climbing a ladder. Ultimately we will reach the step on the ladder that we have desired to attain through God's grace and our patience.

In the Bible we can see examples of those who drove a vehicle that harmonized with their unique God-given personality. One of the best illustrations would be King Jehu who reigned over the northern ten tribes of Israel. The aspect that's so remarkable about Jehu's character and mannerisms is that he was the one who overthrew Jezebel when she seemed almost impossible to defeat. In order to accomplish this prophetic task, he needed to drive fast and furious, and that can't be done with a ride that's known for having horrible acceleration. To properly end the reign of evil queen Jezebel you need to drive something that makes the enemy nervous.

> So the watchman reported, saying, "He went up to them and is not coming back; and the driving is like the driving of Jehu the son of Nimshi, for he drives furiously!" (2 Kings 9:20)

I like the next translation even more, because it reveals that God works through all different types of personalities. I'm certainly not encouraging anyone to break the law through speeding or reckless driving, but what Jehu exhibited was an *attitude of intolerance* against idolatry and the silencing of the prophets. We need this same grace to be poured out within the church today. Anything that you tolerate will never leave your life. Without this type of attitude Jezebel stays on the throne and continues to shut down the prophets of God, the true prophetic flow, and the spiritual gifts that are so necessary in setting people free.

The lookout reported, "He has reached them, but he isn't coming back either. The driving is like that of Jehu son of Nimshi—he drives like a maniac" (2 Kings 9:20 NIV).

Jezebel was married to Ahab, the king of Israel. Together they ruled with domineering and deceitful tactics that served their own personal and selfish interests. Much like some of today's politicians, they tolerated corruption for the sake of financial gain. Behind the scenes it was Jezebel who incited her husband to use any means necessary to achieve wealth, power, and fame. Backroom deals consisting of bribery, extortion, the use of murder, and executive cover-ups in the public eye were tools used extensively by Ahab and Jezebel. Jezebel was cunning and ruthless and strove tirelessly to establish her pagan ideologies upon the Jewish people. She was the manipulative power behind her husband.

There was never anyone like Ahab, who sold himself to do evil in the eyes of the Lord, urged on by Jezebel his wife (1 Kings 21:25 NIV).

Jezebel was the daughter of the wealthy Phoenician King Ethball of Tyre. She was not Jewish by birth but was married to Ahab through a political alliance that benefitted the northern Kingdom of Israel and Phoenicia (now known as Lebanon). While the southern Kingdom of Judah followed Yahweh as the one and true God, the ten northern tribes constantly worshiped multiple gods, particularly the golden calf statues that were set up in the towns of Bethel and Dan. Jezebel was a devout worshiper of Baal and Asherah. Baal was the male god who was the head of fertility and agriculture. Asherah was a female moon goddess who was represented by a tree or a wooden pole, often carved into an image of a woman. Jezebel was determined to stomp out all worship of Yahweh. This meant systematically killing the prophets of the Lord.

For so it was, while Jezebel massacred the prophets of the Lord, that Obadiah had taken one hundred prophets and hidden them, fifty to a cave, and had fed them with bread and water (1 Kings 18:4).

According to the first-century Jewish historian Josephus, the father of Jezebel (King Ethball) served as a priest of Astarte. The Canaanites worshiped Astarte, who was known to the Phoenicians as Asherah, the same goddess but with a slightly different name depending upon the region. Most likely Jezebel was trained from a young age to serve as a high priestess of Baal. She provided government support for 450 prophets of Baal and 400 prophets of Asherah. The role of her wearing makeup and putting on a headdress was more than just the typical cosmetic treatment that many women of the ancient world performed. What Jezebel was doing was a ceremonial religious act that involved ritual prostitution and witchcraft.

Now when Jehu had come to Jezreel, Jezebel heard of it; and she put paint on her eyes and adorned her head, and looked through a window (2 Kings 9:30).

Jezebel was making a last ditch effort to seduce Jehu. She had seduced many others into immorality through the teaching she had instituted through the false prophets. The spirit of Jezebel still operates against the church today through the many forms of media that are saturated with sexual immorality, which are placed before God's people. A Jezebel spirit primarily seeks to manipulate others into sensuality and idolatry.

Nevertheless I have a few things against you, because you allow that woman Jezebel, who calls herself a prophetess, to teach and seduce My servants to commit sexual immorality and eat things sacrificed to idols (Revelation 2:20).

The name of the woman referred to here by Jesus as Jezebel was probably not her real name but was rather a reference to Jezebel of the Old Testament. This woman within the church of Thyatira was endeavoring to establish her authority and influence over the church just as Jezebel tried to do over Israel. The false prophetess mentioned was a woman who had accepted the teachings of the Nicolaitans. This same deceitful message that afflicted the church in the capital city of Ephesus had spread to the church in Pergamos and seems to have been a movement that spread widely throughout the church in Asia Minor.

> But I have a few things against you, because you have there those who hold the doctrine of Balaam, who taught Balak to put a stumbling block before the children of Israel, to eat things sacrificed to idols, and to commit sexual immorality. Thus you also have those who hold the doctrine of the Nicolaitans, which thing I hate (Revelation 2:14-15).

The false prophetess in the church of Thyatira had told the believers it was OK to eat foods sacrificed to idols. She also encouraged sexual immorality and seems to have presented a "boys will be boys" mentality to justify the immoral behavior. This was no doubt intertwined with the Nicolaitan philosophy that sexual promiscuity was not a worldly sin but was only a physical act that did not involve the "inner" act of the soul or spirit; therefore, it was fine to have sex with anyone you wanted.

The Nicolaitans believed that once you grew out of the spiritual babyhood stage that you would then develop into maturity and be able to grasp the "deep things of God." Their teaching emphasized that it really didn't matter what you did with your body. If you eat food sacrificed to idols then it's no big deal because food is a physical thing. They believed that having sex with multiple partners was OK because these were things done in the physical body, and they viewed the physical as unimportant. Their so-called "new revelation" also included the teaching that there wasn't any real thing as ethics or morals. You just had to be true to your "inner self" and not be concerned with any "external" actions. It was this seductive element of the false prophetess's heresy that brought upon her the disgraced name of Jezebel. The Lord Jesus was very patient with this woman and gave her time to repent, but she never did. We must be zealous like Jehu to rid any effects of Jezebel from our lives.

> *Now when he departed from there, he met Jehonadab the son of Rechab, coming to meet him; and he greeted him and said to him, "Is your heart right, as my heart is toward your heart?"*

> *And Jehonadab answered, "It is."*

> *Jehu said, "If it is, give me your hand." So he gave him his hand, and he took him up to him into the chariot. Then he said, "Come with me, and see my zeal for the Lord." **So they had him ride in his chariot** (2 Kings 10:15-16).*

Riding in your own nice chariot (vehicle) can prove to be a tremendous source of motivation to live a holy life. Within your vehicle you can read your Bible during your lunch break at work. You can listen to a biblical teaching message as you drive along. You can pick up a friend and take them to church or to a Christian conference. When God gives you a nice chariot, you don't want to pick up Jezebel with it; you want to run over the devil's temptation through the power of the Holy Spirit.

> *And he [Jehu] looked up at the window, and said, "Who is on my side? Who?" So two or three eunuchs looked out at him. Then he said, "Throw her down." So they threw her down, and some of her blood spattered on the wall and*

on the horses; and he trampled her underfoot (2 Kings 9:32-33).

Jehu ran over Jezebel with his chariot. Then he put it in reverse and backed up and did it again. The body of evil Jezebel was broken and shattered as the war horses pounded her into the ground with their mighty hooves. Witnesses said they heard praise music blasting from Jehu's stereo while he skillfully maneuvered his chariot. Jezebel's evil reign of terror was finished. Of course, when we refer to Jezebel in our modern-day culture we are not directly referring to a person but more to an evil spirit that originally worked through the woman Jezebel and who now works against God's people. To rid Jezebel from your life you can't be passive, but you must be zealous and fiercely driven to live a life of purity and passion for God. Anything that supports you in your quest to walk close with God should be viewed as a blessing and not as a burden. A good chariot (vehicle) is an effective tool in serving the Lord on multiple platforms. In order to use your faith for an exceptional vehicle I suggest you apply the following steps that I have laid out for you, which are my *nine keys to unlocking a heart's desire vehicle.*

NINE KEYS TO UNLOCKING A HEART'S DESIRE VEHICLE

Key 1. Select the vehicle that you want. Tell the Lord in your prayer time which vehicle you want by identifying the make, model, color, and any other available options that you may want included. You must be specific. Then ask the Lord for this precise vehicle. Jesus loves it when we are clear cut and don't mince words, as seen in the following statement, "*So Jesus answered and said to him, 'What do you want Me to do for you?' The blind man said to Him, 'Rabboni, that I may receive my sight'*" (Mark 10:51).

Key 2. Obtain a brochure of the vehicle. This can be done on the Internet or by visiting the dealership. Circle the specific options of your choice. Place this brochure in a place where you will regularly see it. You may want to carry it in your briefcase everywhere you go. Every time you see your brochure say, "Jesus, thank You for my new car (or truck, etc.)."

Key 3. Write on the brochure the date of when you asked God in prayer for this vehicle. If you choose to do this again in the future for another vehicle, you will notice that the second go-around will take less time because your faith will have been developed through experience.

Key 4. Believe now that you have received your new vehicle. Faith believes that it has received before it is ever seen. In your heart, see yourself possessing this vehicle now. As Jesus instructed, "Therefore I say to you, whatever things you ask when you pray, *believe that you receive them, and you will have them*" (Mark 11:24).

Key 5. Dance in advance. What would your reaction be if someone came up to you unexpectedly right now and said, "Let's go, I want to buy you the car of your dreams!" Would you shout? Would you dance? Would you praise God? Anybody can praise God for what they can feel, hear, or see. It doesn't require any faith to do that. You don't need to believe for something that has manifested. At that point you no longer have to believe for it because then you would know it by seeing it. But it takes faith to praise God when your miracle has not yet manifested in the natural realm. Feelings are not required to validate faith. Your works give evidence of your faith. Even if you don't feel like it, jump up right now and dance around your room and begin to praise God for your new vehicle. (Repeat this step often, preferably several times each week.)

Key 6. Embrace the truth that maturity is the ability to delay gratification. Don't rush the process of genuine faith. God is the author of financial wisdom. He doesn't want you to jeopardize your future through an ill-timed purchase. Timing is very important in the kingdom of God. Immature people always believe they must have it now, or else they aren't happy. Be mature and make your purchase wisely. If you plan on financing your vehicle, then pay down your debts and wait until your credit score is very high. Then you can qualify for an acceptable interest rate or a noninterest loan. If you plan on paying cash, then be patient, keep saving, and be continually praising God for those unexpected blessings that significantly help propel you to acquiring the full amount needed.

Key 7. Sow financial seed for the harvest of an exceptional vehicle. For instance, you could purchase a gift certificate from the local car wash and present it to the man or woman of God in your life. That way their car stays clean all of the time, just as you're going to want yours to be. Offer to pay for their oil change or buy them a prepaid gas card that can be used at a Shell, Exxon, or similar gas station. Be creative with your seed sowing.

Key 8. When the miracle is fully manifested and you are holding the keys in your hand to your exceptional vehicle, be sure to tell others of the great things that God has done for you. When Jesus delivered the former demon-possessed man, He told him, "Go home to your friends, and *tell them what great things the Lord has done for you*, and how He has had compassion on you" (Mark 5:19). Don't hide your blessing. Don't apologize for your blessing. You never, ever have to apologize for anything that God does. Enjoy your blessing and thank God constantly for it.

Key 9. Last but not least—go last. Husbands, if your wife is driving a Yugo or a Pontiac Aztek, it's not time for you to drive a new Mercedes Benz. Your wife should experience the same level of comfort and luxury (if not more) than what you would expect to enjoy. Put her first. Use your faith and all of your available resources to get her into a car that makes her happy and thoroughly satisfied. Once you've accomplished this then you can think about what you would like to get. If, however, the man or woman of God in your life is driving a Chevy Chevette, then don't even think about getting a new car until your minister is taken care of. Team together with other church members and ministry partners and get them out of that Chevette and perhaps into a new Corvette just as quick as you can. Or get them a new Cadillac or whatever would delight their heart. If you intentionally go last through the art of serving, you will be pleasantly surprised at what an unusually good thing God will do for you when it's time for you to go up and get your blessing.

Chapter Twelve

Faith to Wrestle with God

Certain blessings of God can require much prayer to step into even as we apply the full force of faith. Consider the subject of revival, for instance. Before the Azusa Street revival broke out in Los Angeles in the early 1900s, the man William Seymour was to be found in fervent prayer. Dr. John G. Lake commented that he spoke with Mr. Seymour before the flames of revival fell at Azusa Street. He said that Brother Seymour had confided in him that he prayed for five hours each day. Later, when the revival was in full swing Brother Seymour was praying seven hours a day. Sometimes we want great results with only a limited amount of personal investment, but great blessings can often be traced to great sacrifices upon the altar of prayer. There are times when prayer can become so intense that it takes the form of wrestling. This can be necessary when it is time for the birthing of a promise of God within your life.

There was a pivotal point in Jacob's life that transitioned him into being the man called by God to birth a nation. Jacob had swindled his older brother Esau, and everyone, including himself, was aware of his glaring and flawed integrity.

> *So he said, "Isn't he rightly named Jacob? For he has cheated me twice now. He took my birthright, and look, now he has taken my blessing"* (Genesis 27:36 HCSB).

Jacob's character deficiencies had come around full circle to face him with divine reckoning. It was time for a change. A change of behavior, even the change of his name. But it wasn't going to happen without there being some wrestling over the outcome. I remember a certain Christian businessman in my community who was notorious for swindling people out of their hard-earned money. This man would prophesy over people, pray for people, speak in tongues in Christian meetings, and then turn right around and lie, cheat, and steal from God's own people. But one day I ran into him at the local post office, and he looked absolutely wiped out. When I inquired what was wrong with him due to his sunken countenance and dismal appearance, he responded by telling me that he had just been swindled out of $400,000. This money was all the savings that he and his wife had, and they had hoped to build their dream home with this money. But now it was all gone, and the worst part was that the husband never told his wife that he had invested all of their savings and that he had lost it to a charlatan more unscrupulous than himself. As his wife sat at home looking at house plans she was still unaware that they had no money in the bank to buy a new sofa, much less a new house. The swindler had finally met his match. He got outfoxed by a greater trickster than himself, and for the first time he was able to experience the same feelings of anxiety and despair as those he had defrauded. It was a sobering reality for him. Several millennia before him we see that Jacob was also facing the same inner turmoil of someone who had gained rewards through unlawful methods.

Whether its exaggerating on a job resume, falsely altering a college transcript, cheating on tests or exams, or lying in order to take a shortcut to the top, eventually there will be a moment of realization when a person sees that they are grossly deficient when stacked against those who followed the proper chain of command. This is why some ministers have *spiritual gravity*—because they paid the full price and refused to take shortcuts. When John Wesley ministered to large crowds outdoors that numbered in the thousands, some of the men would climb up into the trees to get a better view of him as he spoke. John Wesley would tell the men to climb down from the trees or else they would fall out of them when the power of the Holy Spirit began to move. Those who didn't come down ended up falling. This type of ministry is due to *spiritual gravity*.

When George Whitefield preached the gospel the crowds of people would shake, burst into weeping, and fall to the floor as though dead. After traveling from England and across the Atlantic Ocean to preach in Philadelphia, Benjamin Franklin estimated that Whitefield's voice was so forceful that it could be heard by 30,000 people without a microphone and from over a mile away. Whitefield delivered over 18,000 sermons to 10,000,000 people in his lifetime. You can't be a spiritual phony and be a spiritual giant at the same time. True spiritual power is entrusted to those who have wrestled with God and have been changed through divine encounters.

Jacob was now learning the bitter lessons of being dishonest for unfairly taking advantage of others through deceit. Before, he saw no difficulty in cheating his older brother, but when he met Laban, his father-in-law, he met a con man who repeatedly tricked him over and over, forcing Jacob to see a reflection of himself through the actions of Laban. Jacob had worked seven years to acquire Laban's daughter Rachel as his wife. At the end of seven years, Jacob went to collect his pay and basically said, "Uncle Laban, I've worked my time, now please give me Rachel so we may, uhmm, commence with the consummating." Laban agreed to honor the terms and the wedding was planned. There would first be a few days of feasting and dancing in which the bride would be heavily veiled during these festivities. Finally, after the reading of the marriage contract, Jacob would have taken his bride into the marriage tent, which in our modern day would be the start of the honeymoon vacation. They would spend their first night together cloaked in darkness. After seven years of romantic longing, I'm sure there were some heavily pent up emotions that night. The two honeymooners probably didn't get much sleep as they explored their newfound depths of love for each other. Jacob finally got the woman of his dreams—Rachel, the prettiest girl in town. He fell off to sleep with a profound sense of contentment.

When he awoke the next morning, his world was shaken by what he saw. There lying next to him was not Rachel but Leah, the older sister. I know what you're thinking. How in the world could any guy not notice that the woman he is in bed with is some other woman than his wife? Just as Jacob and his mother Rebecca had years earlier plotted together to trick Isaac by rehearsing what to say and what not to say in order to manipulate Isaac, I believe similarly that Laban coached Leah to do the same thing. Laban probably said to Leah, "Don't speak any words; that way Jacob will never know until the morning. And stay away from the moonlight so he can't see you. In the morning it will have been too late because he will already have slept with you, thus making the marriage binding."

Jacob could hardly fathom his situation as he awakened. He realized Laban had pulled the old bait and switch tactic on him. How did Laban explain the unorthodox situation? He simply argued that "It must not be done so in our country, to give the younger before the firstborn" (Gen. 29:26). What's so ironic about this chapter of Jacob's life is that the reason for the switch is because of *birthright*. Years earlier, Jacob deceitfully took away his brothers *birthright*, and now he experiences the same feeling of being deprived through a legal loophole exploited by Laban. Touché for Laban as he executed a crafty move for the well-being of his family, as well as unknowingly serving a classic dish of sowing and reaping that Jacob was forced to swallow.

Laban was not done, however, with extracting all he could from Jacob, so he offered him a bargain deal of also lawfully acquiring Rachel as his wife (along with Leah who now belonged to him), all for the unbelievably low price of just seven more years of labor. When the second round of seven years were complete things were still not rosy between Jacob and Laban. After the fourteen years were completed, Jacob stayed around for another six more years, hoping things would get better. But after a total of twenty years of working for Laban, Jacob had finally reached the point where he knew this relationship with Laban was not stacked in his favor. Jacob sat down to have a heart-to-heart talk with Leah and Rachel and to discuss the possibility of leaving and going back to Canaan.

> *And you know that with all my might I have served your father. Yet your father has deceived me and changed my wages ten times, but God did not allow him to hurt me* (Genesis 31:6-7).

In a surprising show of unity, Leah and Rachel were in complete agreement with each other and with Jacob. At this point Jacob decided to hightail it out of town with his two wives, sons, and all of their possessions and livestock. Laban was off shearing his sheep, and it wasn't until three days later that he was told the news. After a seven-day pursuit Laban and his guys caught up with Jacob's caravan. Here things were emotionally sorted out between Jacob and Laban through a verbal vent of accumulated frustration. Once things were talked through and tempers receded, a covenant was established between the two. Laban left early the next morning to return to his place, and Jacob was now positioned to soon step into a new chapter in his life. But before this could happen he had to seek the forgiveness of his brother Esau and try to restore the damaged relationship.

Jacob found himself journeying in the desert with his group, and he received word by a messenger that Esau and his 400 men were coming to pay him a visit. In Jacob's mind, he perceived that this visit was not to have tea and scones or to discuss pleasant childhood memories; rather, Esau was approaching to take revenge upon him for his deceitful act of stealing the blessing of the birthright. In response, Jacob feared for his life. He sent his servants and family ahead of him and across the brook Jabbok in an effort to establish as much buffer as possible between Esau and his family. Jacob stayed alone so he could discuss his predicament with God. The following short phrase reveals an insight into an ongoing truth that still seeks to tug at our heart today.

> He took them and sent them across the stream. And he sent across whatever he had. Then Jacob was left alone (Genesis 32:23-24 NASB).

It's important to position yourself at times so that you can be alone with God. When you get alone there are two distinct voices that will often speak to you. The first voice that wants to speak is your con-science. What is your conscience? Your conscience is the voice of your spirit. You are a spirit, you have a soul, and you live in your body (see 1 Thess. 5:23). Some people don't want to get alone because they know there is debris they have swept beneath the carpet of their hearts, and if they ever get alone and quiet then their conscience will convict them. As a Christian, if you tell a lie or exaggerate then your conscience will convict you. If you treat someone wrong or unfairly you will know on the inside. When we walk in constant fellowship with our Lord and are quick to repent then we can stand before God with a clear conscience.

> Paul, looking intently at the Council, said, "Brethren, I have lived my life with a perfectly good conscience before God up to this day" (Acts 23:1 NASB).

Often people cover up their conscience with lots of activity, particularly nonstop talking. They have to be constantly doing something lest their conscience speak to them of certain wrongs they have committed. Some time back I was riding in an airplane for a short domestic flight, seated in the middle of a plane that had about fifty rows of seats. The flight lasted less than two hours, and from the moment we took off till the moment we landed a lady sitting on the very last row talked nonstop and so loud that seventy percent of the plane could hear every word she said. The grieved expression written on the faces of the people toward the rear of the plane was, "When is that person going to stop talking?!" After the plane deboarded and we caught our connecting gate for our next flight, my wife and I happened to see this same woman walking through the airport terminal still talking to someone so loud and so fast that we wondered if she ever stopped to even breathe. Never once did she take an intermission; her conscience was smothered by a hard heart that had become calloused to sin.

The world is getting louder and louder. For example, if you watch or attend a basketball game, you notice the transformation to nonstop entertainment. The moment the players call a timeout there is a man in the audio sound booth who pushes a button and immediately blaring music begins to play. Digital billboards within the arena flash and quickly change from one advertisement to another while the scoreboard acts as one giant television with more color and visual stimulation. The whole event is a continual entertainment act that is designed to not give the audience a moment to blink. Sporting events have become total sensory overload experiences. The corrupt world system tries hard to keep you busy, engaged, entertained, and in a constant loud mode. But we must find time to become quiet.

Jacob was now alone. The second voice that wanted to speak was the voice of God. When God comes around, He may not want to initially launch into your list of questions that you have waiting for Him.

He may just want to "hang out" for a while and enjoy your company. There have been times in my prayer life when I have asked God certain questions, and the Lord has directly spoken to me and said, "I don't want to talk about that right now." Who am I to dictate the mood of the Lord of the entire universe? I simply go with His flow. Who knows? He may not be much in the mood for explaining what caused the dinosaurs to go extinct, but He may feel like it would be a great time for you and Him to wrestle. You just go with His agenda. The purpose for why He comes by is because He wants to transform you more into His glorious image. Are you ready for a deeper change—are you ready to wrestle with God? Often wrestling precedes a new anointing, a new breakthrough, and a new revelation of God.

> *Then Jacob was left alone, and a man wrestled with him until daybreak. When he saw that he had not prevailed against him, he touched the socket of his thigh; so the socket of Jacob's thigh was dislocated while he wrestled with him. Then he said, "Let me go, for the dawn is breaking." But he said, "I will not let you go unless you bless me." So he said to him, "What is your name?" And he said, "Jacob." He said, "Your name shall no longer be Jacob, but Israel; for you have striven with God and with men and have prevailed"* (Genesis 32:24–28 NASB).

This is unusual to see Jacob wrestling. Esau was clearly more of a physically fit person; the Bible describes him as a skillful hunter who was quite hairy and could easily be seen in our minds as the rough and rugged person who would excel in any type of strength competition. But Jacob was the exact opposite, being a mild man who lived in tents and did not like the idea of outdoor camping like his brother did. Jacob would have much preferred spending a day at the library instead of rock climbing or swimming across rivers. Yet we find Jacob entering into an all-night wrestling match with the Lord. You may not consider yourself to be a "prayer intercessor," but there can arise such a hunger for change in your life that you would do something drastically out of your normal mode of behavior to achieve it. Sometimes the pressures we face in life can drive us into a divine wrestling match. For Jacob, the thought of waking up the next morning and having his brother take revenge by killing him and his family was enough to inspire him to abandon sleep and step into the wrestling ring. Other factors certainly influenced his willingness to wrestle—primarily the longing for a fresh start, to somehow be rid of the identity of being a con man, and to ultimately be blessed.

The wrestling match continued just until the breaking of dawn. Jacob's hip had been dislocated by God, and now he couldn't properly generate leverage. Clinging to the feet of his antagonist, he refused to let go until he received a blessing.

> And He said, "Let Me go, for the day breaks." But he said, "I will not let You go unless You bless me!" So He said to him, "What is your name?" He said, "Jacob." And He said, "Your name shall no longer be called Jacob, but Israel; for you have struggled with God and with men, and have prevailed" (Genesis 32:26-28).

Jacob's tenacity to receive the blessing was clearly pleasing to the Lord. A blessing was then pronounced on Jacob, "Your name shall no longer be called Jacob [deceiver], but Israel [he who strives with God]." The Lord didn't let Jacob's past failures or mistakes define him, and He won't let yours either. He forgave Jacob of his sins and no longer held them against him. His grace and forgiveness are made abundantly available to us. This time Jacob got the blessing the *right way* without the involvement of any deception. He didn't use steroids or performance-enhancing drugs before stepping onto the wrestling mat to gain an unlawful edge. He fought for it fair and square and was even injured in the process. He applied an unrelenting faith that caused him to prevail in the end.

What blessing do you want and need from God at this season in your life? How much do you really want it? You can have it, but you may have a few nights where you don't get as much sleep as you would prefer. You can have the blessing, but you may limp afterward. Jacob walked with a limp for the rest of his life, but that's OK because he had no future plans of entering the Olympic high jump competition. It was more important for him to have God's blessing. We must embrace this same understanding.

Through Jacob's story we can see that wrestling can be associated with prayer through biblical symbolism. Even if it demands intense prayer, it's worth whatever it takes to cause the blessing of God to be released. When I wrote my first book years back, I also purchased several thousand copies of it for my ministry that I could sell during my itinerant travels. When my first bill came in for the books I had purchased, I saw that I owed an initial payment of $5,000. As the due date grew nearer for the payment to be made, I still did not have the money. I was able to pay my own normal bills, but for some reason I never had an extra $5,000 come in to cover this small bill. It finally came down to the day before the due date when I decided I needed to do a little wrestling with God. Unlike Jacob, my wrestling match was not at night but early in the morning. I explained my predicament to God in detail, sharing with Him my need to walk in integrity and always pay my bills on time because I am an ambassador for Him. I also told the Lord how I mentioned in my book that He causes angels to assist in bringing financial support. Endeavoring to relay to the Lord my concern, I said, "Lord, how can I write a book called *Working with Angels* in which I mention how Your angels help with finances, and then be late on the very bill for my copies of this book?" As I prayed it seemed as if a weighty burden came upon me to see God deliver me from my financial shortage, caused by the enemy not wanting me to break through to a new level by becoming an established Christian author. I prayed strongly, just as a wrestler would sweat and exert energy, until I felt a "release" in my spirit. After almost two hours of wrestling in prayer, I sensed a breakthrough in the Spirit and I knew that God was going to work it out somehow.

Later that morning, a local elderly couple called me and asked if I could come by their house and pray for the wife who was battling cancer. Often I had dropped by to minister to them and particularly share a faith-building message with the woman who was sick. These were times of one-on-one ministry. They were a precious married couple who were both retired and living on a very limited income. I had never expected to receive any monetary benefit from my visits because I knew they were financially constrained. I taught the dear lady for 45 minutes from the Word of God, at which time she thanked me and then I returned home.

As my day progressed I went by the post office to see if any ministry donations had come in, but there weren't any. No phone calls came in, no e-mails arrived, and any possible source of help was nowhere to be found. Before I knew it the sun was setting and the day was over. The money was still due the next day. My faith was tested, but something from the previous wrestling match continued to allow me to sense victory. At 9:00 at night my phone rang and the husband of the sick woman called me and asked if I would please come over to their house and teach them another Bible message. I thought, "That's interesting, at 9:00 at night you want another message?" While his request seemed to be a little bit unusual, the idea also came to me that I didn't have anything else to do so I might as well go.

When I arrived it was about 9:20 P.M., and as I came in the husband and wife were sitting together on their couch and were smiling.

The husband said, "Steven, we didn't really want you to teach another lesson tonight, we just wanted to have you come over so we could surprise you." The husband continued by saying, "Today an overdue retirement check was wire transferred into my bank account. You have been such a blessing to us that we wanted to also give you a blessing. On the fireplace mantle is a check for you in the amount of 5,000 dollars. Thank you for ministering God's Word to us. Please use this gift in whatever way you would like."

It was a joy to pay my bill on time the next day. Sometimes I think about what certain outcomes would have been, in the many pressure situations that life has hurled at me, if I had not gotten out on the wrestling mat and met the Lord in the center of the ring. Because I chose to pray, embarrassment was replaced with accolades, apparent loss was turned to victory, and the devil was denied while God was highly exalted. Years back, my pastor faced a tremendous challenge when his oldest daughter returned from the hospital after receiving her first ultrasound of her baby. The doctor showed them the images that revealed the baby was nothing more than a blob of physical tissue. As the pregnancy progressed, the ultrasound images verified that the "blob" was unchanged. There were no visible arms, legs, eyes, or any normal developing body parts. My pastor prayed and never let up in wrestling as he refused to let the devil get away with such a hideous attack upon his daughter's baby.

When the day finally came for the "blob" to be born, out popped the most beautiful little girl you could imagine! The doctor was shocked. People were stunned. But my pastor was full of praise and thanksgiving because he believed God was going to do a miracle. Today, the former "blob" is a beautiful teenage young lady who is excelling in all of her high school activities. There is a lifestyle of winning that is gained through spiritual wrestling that is so sweet and rewarding that you wish everyone could share in it. Potentially, every

Christian can—but it starts by getting alone. If you will make the effort to get alone then He will show up and engage you with what is on His heart, and you can talk also about what's on your heart as well. The Lord is deeply interested in fulfilling your needs and deepest desires. Like Jacob, whose name was changed to Israel, may you also experience God's transforming power through heaven's form of wrestling—unrelenting prayer.

Chapter Thirteen

ENJOYING YOUR BLESSINGS IN THE PEACE OF GOD

*Be anxious for nothing, but in everything by prayer
and supplication, with thanksgiving, let your
requests be made known to God; and the peace of
God, which surpasses all understanding, will guard
your hearts and minds through Christ Jesus.*
—PHILIPPIANS 4:6-7

In order to possess and enjoy the blessings of God we must have a calm spirit. We are commanded in the Scripture not to be anxious about anything. Anxiety is capable of stealing our joy that is meant to be attached to the blessings of God. To be "anxious" in the original Greek language means to be "troubled with care." God does not want you to be troubled, worried, or anxious about any of the daily difficulties and problems you face in your life. When feelings of anxiety begin to try to come upon you, then it is necessary to pray to stay in the divine comfort zone of God's peace. If we don't pray, then it's easy for the cares and concerns of our lives to leave us in a place of stress and feeling overwhelmed. Prayer is the antidote to stay in peace. When we linger with God in prayer and cast our cares on Him, then we are refreshed and strengthened. Without peace our blessings, no matter how wonderful they are, simply cannot be appreciated.

I know a man who is a tremendous leader in his respected career field. While those around him see him as bulletproof and invincible, he secretly has an Achilles heel that requires that he must strongly lean on the Lord for grace. His hidden weakness is panic attacks, although those he leads have no idea of his kryptonite weakness. By me teaching him how to pray daily and integrate some fasting into his life, he completely overcame these debilitating attacks. But he also realized that he must continue to pray and walk close to the Lord to live in ongoing freedom. Because he discovered that a rich prayer life is the key to peace he can now enjoy his work without any fear or anxiety.

When we pray we are also instructed to use supplications. Supplications are requests we make to God during our times of seeking Him in prayer. In the New Testament Greek language, the word for "supplication" could also be understood as "asking God for something that you want or need." As we pray and converse with God about our needs, desires, and special requests, we will be transported into a peaceful haven. It is important to take the time necessary for this process to work itself out. We all want to perpetually experience the peace of God that goes beyond our understanding. But I've found that I can't sustain that peace unless my prayer time reaches a certain measure of fulfillment.

There's no specific set of rules for the time needed to enter into this tranquil place of deep peace. A lot of it most likely depends on our current situation involving the events taking place in our daily life. If there are many pressures weighing against you then it will most likely take more time than normal to be clothed with complete peace. We must be willing to stay on our knees until we reach this threshold where the anxiety is dissipated and we once again experience a fresh infilling of the Holy Spirit. To leave prematurely from the secret place of prayer only causes us to live our lives below the kingdom level of wholeness that God intends for us to walk in.

As we pray with a thankful heart, we enter into a place where we make supplication. We open our hearts to God and speak freely with Him. At this place we share with Him the requests that are heavy on our hearts, as the Scripture says, "let your requests be made known to God." The word *requests* is plural, so it reveals that we can often have more than one thing that we are making a request for. The Greek word for "request" is the word *aitema* and it means "to ask in such a way that you will not take no for an answer." In other words, it is a bold request, a strong petition, with a determination to get exactly what you are asking. We see a great example of this in the following Scripture.

> But they were insistent, demanding with loud voices that
> He be crucified. And the voices of these men and of the chief
> priests prevailed. So Pilate gave sentence that it should be as
> they requested (Luke 23:23-24).

We see the word *requested* (*aitema* in the Greek) being used in a negative way by the Jewish crowd and religious leaders to achieve what they wanted with an attitude of not accepting anything from Pilate other than what they have requested. In a positive way we want to approach God with thankful hearts that are also full of faith. We want to pray according to His will and make our requests known to Him with expectancy to receive the very thing we are asking for. This reflects that we are serious about our prayers being answered. When you enter into this deep level of prayer you move into the realm of the Holy Spirit. When you are in the Spirit you are no longer anxious. It is impossible for the Holy Spirit to be anxious, so when we are in Him then we are in the peace of God.

Sometimes when praying you can feel or discern the exact moment when anxiety lifts off of you. When you experience this, it is not the ideal time to get up and leave your prayer closet. Rather, continue a while further in prayer and become clothed with the Spirit, pushing back all cares and concerns. Unload any spiritual baggage that you may be carrying. The peace of God will flood your heart and form a protective garrison around your heart and mind. When the needed amount of prayer focus has been expended upon the specific request, then you will feel a type of lightness within your heart. You will notice you are no longer heavy and troubled about things. It may take an hour to reach this state, but whether its thirty minutes or an hour or even longer, it's well worth the time spent. Not only do you receive immediate refreshing but you have pressed through toward the primary goal of God granting your request to you.

God is able to alleviate our difficulties through prayer and fully resolve all troubling issues. It is possible for some Christians to miss out on the delivering power of prayer because they are currently suppressed with so many dilemmas. One of the main encumbrances to prayer is what we all know as "discouragement." The problems and varied difficulties of life can have a way of eroding away our exuberance to win. Over time it is possible for a believer to lose their passion and purpose and thus slip into a mode of discouragement. It's hard to get out of bed when you are discouraged. When it seems your prayers are going unanswered and life has passed you by, then there can be a direct loss of motivation and momentum.

For example, if a person is physically sick and is struggling financially then they may lie in bed in the morning and think, "What's the use of even trying to pray? Nothing ever changes or gets better for me. My body is in pain and I am drowning in debt." However, most of them still find a way to get up in time to get ready for work because if they don't work then there will be a total collapse of peace by having no money for food or a place to live. So a person moves forward by necessity, even if it's done grudgingly and with much sadness in their heart. The Lord Jesus doesn't want you to be discouraged. Often I receive e-mails from people requesting that I pray for them to win the lottery. These are from Christians who feel overwhelmed with the troubles of life and are looking for a shortcut to financial relief. In their discouragement they often become desperate and use what little money they have to make undisciplined spending decisions such as buying lottery tickets. When we look to the Lord Jesus in faith and begin to operate by His financial principles, then we begin to walk on the path of stability and peace.

Once a prayer method is established it's easy to maintain and it will form a barrier against discouragement and other negative feelings. To assist in pushing away discouragement so that you may take your place of establishing an uninterrupted flow of daily prayer and communion with God, I have listed a few insightful verses along with my recommended *seven strong pillars of successful prayer.*

SEVEN STRONG PILLARS OF SUCCESSFUL PRAYER

*However, the report went around concerning Him all the more; and great multitudes came together to hear, and to be healed by Him of their infirmities. So He Himself **often withdrew into the wilderness and prayed** (Luke 5:15-16).*

Pillar 1. Withdraw often to pray. Determine now—no matter how busy you get or how much success you experience, despite how much money you may be making, or how many people are getting saved in a revival—that it is essential that you must often withdraw to pray in a quiet and peaceful place. No matter how good and helpful your works are, even if they are ministry works, you still must not place any work before your devotional life, or else you will eventually burn out.

Pillar 2. Realize that your prayer life is not responsible for saving the whole world. Meditate on that statement, then take a deep breath and relax. Until we get to heaven there will always be sick people and those needing deliverance. There will always be multitudes of lost and unsaved souls who need salvation. It was the same way when the Lord ministered. We must still take time out for proper rest and to spiritually recharge. You are allowed to sleep and rest just as Jesus also did.

> *Then He came to the disciples and found them sleeping, and said to Peter, "What! Could you not watch with Me one hour? Watch and pray lest you enter into temptation. The spirit indeed is willing, but the flesh is weak"* (Matthew 26:40-41).

Pillar 3. Pray for a straight and uninterrupted time period of one hour. I want to encourage you to aim to pray in your prayer sessions for not 20 minutes or 45 minutes but a complete hour to emulate the life of Jesus. Some Christians try to pray for 20 minutes in the morning, then later they'll pray for 20 minutes at lunch, and then before going to sleep they will pray another 20 minutes. But a stop-and-go method can be difficult to establish a rhythm where the anointing can begin to smoothly flow and your prayer time really begins to roll along. Define your prayer goal. Setting an hour goal gives you a target to push for. When we define our goals we are more likely to reach them. Make your target an hour of prayer. It appears Jesus was referring to one solid hour of uninterrupted prayer. I believe this is the best pattern we should follow concerning timed segments of prayer.

Pillar 4. Winning is one of the greatest motivators. In light of that, please understand that if you skip your prayer time you could suffer unnecessary defeat. Nobody likes to lose. Jesus told His disciples to watch and pray so that they would not enter into temptation. Without an active prayer life, you may enter into something out of weakness or a poor choice. Not praying will leave you vulnerable to your weak human nature. You may then find yourself having wandered into a cave full of sleeping lions. What should you do then? Preferably you should back out just as quietly as possible and hope none of them suddenly wake up. It's better never to experience those types of situations. Prayer is both offensive and defensive. It keeps you in God's protection and places a shield of angelic guard all around you. The world is a sinful and dangerous place. You can't afford to not pray.

Pillar 5. Be open to the flow of the Holy Spirit carrying you beyond the one-hour mark. Renew your mind to the concept of what could be considered a "long time" in prayer. The Christians today who walk with God like Enoch did in ancient times consider an hour of prayer to be an appetizer. You can have as much of God as you want. Eat until you are full. In other words, pray until you are satisfied, just as you would be full after leaving the table after a Christmas or Thanksgiving meal. Many of the Christians in South Korea have been trained to view an hour of prayer as a comparison to running a lap on a jogging track while they pray the Lord's Prayer (see Matt. 6:9–13). If you have done one lap but wish to do more then you simply keep running for another lap, which would be another hour of prayer, once again praying through the Lord's Prayer.

Pillar 6. You must learn to command your body in order to pray effectively. The flesh does not want to pray. Shortly before Jesus was arrested in the Garden of Gethsemane, He came to His disciples and found them sleeping when they were supposed to be praying. He woke them up and went away to pray a second time. Upon His return, they had fallen back to sleep. After waking them a second time, He left to go back to His time of prayer. Upon returning a third time, He discovered they had all fallen asleep again. But by this time it was too late for the disciples to pray. As tired as they were, they were jolted awake when the large crowd armed with swords and clubs arrived with a loud clamor. Without prayer you can act out of character, as that night the Lord's disciples abandoned Him. Prayer inspires faith and courage. There are times when it will not be easy to pray. You must learn to push yourself. Most people get up in the morning and go to work even if they don't feel like it. This is a part of us accepting our responsibility. We will not always feel like doing what's right, but this is where maturity and discipline have their place of influence. There is tremendous confidence in the Lord when you face problems in a state of having prayed, as compared to not having prayed and thus being caught off guard and unable to respond effectively. Don't let your body be your boss. Train it to get up and go pray.

Pillar 7. Keep a prayer log book to record how much time you spent in prayer each day. This is not necessarily a journal but more of an accounting system that helps you gauge your prayer performance. Just like a checkbook allows you to see where your money is going, a prayer log book will help you balance your time more wisely. The following verse illustrates this principle to us of good record keeping.

> So then each of us will give an account of himself to God (Romans 14:12 NASB).

The context of the above verse speaks of not judging others but of taking personal inventory of our life. When we take inventory, we know exactly how much surplus we have on hand as well as being aware of any deficits that we may be facing. A good inventory eliminates guesswork and gives an accurate measurement of where we truly stand. I truly believe that when you look at someone's checkbook that tracks where their money is spent, you also see a picture of where their heart is. If a person says they deeply love the Lord but there is no record of giving to the Lord's work, then the accounting system will reveal this discrepancy.

When I participated in running on the track team in college, it was mandatory for us to keep a log book that showed how many miles we ran each day and the combined weekly total. (I still have my old mileage log books from college and even high school, believe it or not!) At the end of each week, the head coach would personally review every runner's log book to see if they fulfilled their mileage require-ments. We were the national championship track team, and our coach was considered by some to be the greatest collegiate track coach in the nation. He knew that if we did the specified workouts that he outlined for us we would rise to be winners. He also knew that if we didn't put in the work that he asked of us we wouldn't be able to compete to be the best.

For those of us who were middle distance runners, we were given the weekly standard of running a minimum of 70 miles. Sometimes I exceeded that requirement, and other times I came up short. Either way the coach would make notations giving his insight to help me become better. At this time, I was room-mating with a friend who was my same age. He came to college on a track scholarship after a sterling high school running career in which he was the state cham-pion of New York. He wasn't adjusting well with his transition from New York to Texas, and his performance was suffering. In his great frustration with the unsatisfactory way he was going, he decided to push far beyond the required 70-mile goal. That week he went out and ran 180 miles. He literally ran a marathon every day for seven days in a row. At the end of the week he could hardly walk. There was one particular day of the week a friend and I drove across town and we happened to see him running by himself at a distance of twelve miles away from our dorm room. He really did legitimately put the miles in. When the coach saw his log book he made a notation that said, "I think you have mistakenly recorded the total of your mileage." When it was explained to him that the mileage was accurate, the coach used him as an example before the entire team of someone who was willing to "go the extra mile" in order to win. Two weeks later my friend had a breakout performance and went on to winning success in his running career.

Go out today and purchase for yourself a suitable log book from any type of office supply store. A prayer log book holds you accountable. The numbers (time spent with God) don't lie but speak truthfully about your commitment to walk with God. A prayer log book provides a track record of success that will allow you to virtually show others how you succeeded, and you can use this to motivate others who also need wisdom and guidance in this area. I want you to be mindful that a short pencil is better than a long memory. A log book allows you to express and record certain notes or important revelations that otherwise would be surely lost. And most importantly, a log book shows God that you are serious about your spiritual development. Ten or twenty years from now when you review your old log books, you will be shocked at your progress of growth and development in Christ. Over time these log books will become of more value to you than gold.

As you complete your prayer time, keep in mind that the best witness of the Holy Spirit that confirms a successful prayer time is being overtaken with the peace of God. When this happens you can be assured that you are praying in an accurate and biblical way, which then results in miraculous answers to your prayers.

Chapter Fourteen

ANGELIC WEALTH TRANSFER

I would like to share with you a co-partnering work that is occurring in the earth today to expedite the manifestation of the blessings of God. This unique collaboration is between God's people and His angels, and it has been reserved for the end-time dispensation in which we are living. It's an amazing work that is now being unveiled by the Holy Spirit. Already it is breaking forth in the lives of God's people. We can expect this movement to increase in momentum and eventually culminate in its fullest measure to facilitate the harvest of billions of souls into the kingdom of God through global evangelism and ensuing discipleship. Most importantly, you are called by God to be a participant in this global proceeding in which you and the angelic armies will move together in synchrony to accomplish the will of God concerning the release of unprecedented miracle provision and financial wealth. Let's begin our study of this fascinating end-of-the-age subject by going to a book in the Bible that features a lengthy discussion between the prophet Zechariah and the angels of God.

> *And the Lord answered the angel who talked to me, with good and comforting words. So the angel who spoke with me said to me, "Proclaim, saying, 'Thus says the Lord of hosts: "I am zealous for Jerusalem and for Zion with great*

zeal. I am exceedingly angry with the nations at ease; for I
was a little angry, and they helped—but with evil intent"'"
(Zechariah 1:13–15).

The context of the book of Zechariah is outlined in the first chapter. The Lord is very angry with the nations that are currently at ease
for the way they improperly dealt with Israel as a nation. The Gentile nations of Assyria and Babylon (along with other lesser nations)
were used by God to discipline Israel. But in their rage they went far
beyond the level of discipline that God had intended. God gave them
an inch, but they took a mile. They literally tried to destroy Israel and
remove her from being a recognized nation upon the earth. This has
aroused the anger of God and He plans on bringing judgment against
these nations.

Again proclaim, saying, "Thus says the Lord of hosts: 'My
cities shall again spread out through prosperity; the Lord
will again comfort Zion, and will again choose Jerusalem'"
(Zechariah 1:17).

The Lord promises to bring comfort to His people, who have
been brought low and have suffered so much, by empowering them to
spread out through prosperity. God loves prosperity, and He always
has thoughts on His mind of how He wants to bless you. The Lord is
revealing to us His agony over the situation that His people have been
plundered, plunged into debt, taken advantage of by excessively high
interest rates, raked over the financial coals, and victimized in all fac-
ets of their life by their former captors. The Lord tells the angel what
He is going to do in order to comfort Zion.

For thus says the Lord of hosts: "He sent Me after glory,
to the nations which plunder you; for he who touches you
touches the apple of His eye. For surely I will shake My

*hand against them, and they shall become spoil for their
servants. Then you will know that the Lord of hosts has sent
Me"* (Zechariah 2:8-9).

He sent Me after glory refers to the Lord going after the wealth
of the Gentiles. What is the *glory* of the Gentiles? Is it their ability
to curse or take God's name in vain? Or is it their ability to remove
all knowledge of God from the school and educational systems in
America and turn the country toward socialism? Or perhaps could
their glory be the media's ability to influence a nation to sink into a
complete loss of moral values? No, it's certainly none of these ungodly
characteristics. The *glory* of the Gentiles is their wealth, and Jesus is
going after those who have plundered His people in order to *shake His
hand against them.* If Jesus grabs something and shakes it then it will
be loosed no matter how hard someone may try to cling to it. He is
going to shake the godless world system of finance, and the wealth of
the Gentiles will become spoil for God's people. Spoil is the reward
for winning in war. Nations go to war in order to take spoil. I want you
to catch a glimpse of what is unfolding behind the scenes of the spiritual realm and understand that a battle is being fought between angels
and evil spirits over which men and women upon the earth receive
financial spoil. The Lord has determined that it's time for the enemy's
camp to be plundered.

As we experience this wealth transfer, we will begin to personally
understand the revelation of Jesus as the *Lord of hosts.* Over the past
few decades, through much teaching the church has become familiar
with the various compound names of God, such as *Jehovah Shalom*
(the Lord Who is our Peace) and other variants such as Jehovah Jireh
(Our Provider), *Jehovah Rapha* (Our Healer), *Jehovah Roi* (Our Shep-
herd), and so forth. "The Lord of hosts" refers to the hosts of heaven,
which are the angelic armies. When some Christians hear the phrase
Lord of hosts, they picture Jesus as being a polite host and we are the

ones who are being hosted to enjoy tea and cookies with Him when we get to heaven. But this romanticized idea of the Lord of hosts does not fit the true biblical description concerning the name *Lord of hosts,* which in the Hebrew is *Jehovah Tsaba.* The hosts that are mentioned are the angelic armies. Jesus is the Lord (captain) over the angelic armies, and He oversees His angel armies as they transfer the wealth of sinners and corrupt sources into the hands of His people who walk in proven stewardship of biblical financial principles. It is a responsibility and extraordinary privilege for the end-time church to know Jesus as *Jehovah Tsaba,* the Almighty Warrior who is the captain of the armies of heaven.

> *He also brought them out with silver and gold, and there*
> *was none feeble among His tribes* (Psalm 105:37).

The deliverance of God's people is always associated with mighty signs and wonders. This particular psalm speaks in depth about the Israelites coming out of the bondage of Egypt through the mighty power of God. For those of us who watched the 1956 classic *The Ten Commandments* starring Charlton Heston as Moses, we were struck by the dramatic splitting of the Red Sea. We watched as young and old crossed over, with many struggling to pass through the sea due to old age and sickness. It was a great movie in many ways, but as we know most Christian movies detour greatly from the actual biblical script. When the estimated number of three million Israelites left Egypt, the Word of God tells us that there was not one feeble person among them. This is an epic miracle. No one was limping or crawling or having to be dragged along. Nobody was using an oxygen tank to supplement their air supply. No elderly people were being pushed in wheelchairs or hobbling on crutches. Every single person was supernaturally strengthened to walk under their own power. Healing evangelist Kathryn Kuhlman prophesied in her day that there would be a time in the church before the Lord's return when not one Christian would be sick.

But that's not all that was miraculous concerning the Jews leaving Egypt. Another miracle of unheard-of proportions took place when they left Egypt with the Egyptians' silver and gold and personal belongings. God was performing a double sign to bear witness to the deliverance of His people—the sign of restoration of health and the sign of supernatural transfer of wealth.

> *And I will give this people favor in the sight of the Egyptians; and it shall be, when you go, that you shall not go empty-handed. But every woman shall ask of her neighbor, namely, of her who dwells near her house, articles of silver, articles of gold, and clothing; and you shall put them on your sons and on your daughters. So you shall plunder the Egyptians (Exodus 3:21-22).*

> *Now the children of Israel had done according to the word of Moses, and they had asked from the Egyptians articles of silver, articles of gold, and clothing. And the Lord had given the people favor in the sight of the Egyptians, so that they granted them what they requested. Thus they plundered the Egyptians (Exodus 12:35-36).*

Consider the magnitude of this miracle. All at the same time, without other neighbors, friends, or family members knowing the others' actions, the Egyptians simultaneously were moved to give away their most valuable belongings to the Israelites. This was not staged, rehearsed, or preplanned by the Egyptians. It was spontaneous, and it happened quickly. Just as evil spirits can whisper in the ears of people in an effort to influence people to do wrong, millions of angels must have whispered into the ears of the entire nation of Egypt and to all the Egyptians, influencing them to give away all of their wealth to the Israelites in one day. This is a historic miracle.

In 2003, a prominent Egyptian legal scholar put together a lawsuit against Jews around the world for taking what he calculated to be over a trillion dollars of Egyptian gold during the Jews' departure of Egypt that occurred 3,300 years ago. Nabil Hilmy, dean of the faculty of law at Egypt's Zagazig University, claimed that the Jews stole "from the Pharaonic Egyptians gold, jewelry, cooking utensils, silver ornaments, clothing, and more, leaving Egypt in the middle of the night with all this wealth, which today is priceless." He based his lawsuit on the Scriptures of Exodus 12:35-36. Hilmy said, "If we assume that the weight of what was stolen was one ton," its worth "doubled every 20 years, even if annual interest is only 5 percent...after 1,000 years, it would be worth 1,125,898,240 million tons.... This is for one stolen ton. The stolen gold is estimated at 300 tons, and it was not stolen for 1,000 years, but for 5,758 years, by the Jewish reckoning. Therefore, the debt is very large."[1]

Hilmy said that he has "set up a legal team to prepare the necessary legal confrontation aimed at restoring what the Jews stole a long time ago, to which the statute of limitations cannot possibly apply." Hilmy said that Jews around the world should pay their fair share, especially those living in Israel. He said, "There may be a compromise solution. The debt can be rescheduled over 1,000 years, with the addition of the cumulative interest during that period." Hilmy's case never seems to have made it into an official court outside of the Muslim nations.[2]

Hilmy was obviously unaware that an almost exact claim was made over 2,000 years ago in a type of world court presided over by the famous Alexander the Great.

The story is recounted in Sanhedrin 91a, where it is recorded that one Geviha ben Pesisa responded on the Jews' behalf. A paraphrase of the excerpt follows:

"What is your source?" Geviha asked the Egyptian representatives.

"The Torah," they replied.

"Very well," said Geviha, "I too will invoke the Torah, which says that the Jews spent 430 years laboring in Egypt. Please compensate us for 600,000 men's work for that period of time."

The Egyptians, the Talmud continues, then asked Alexander for three days during which to formulate a response. The recess was granted but the representatives, finding no counter-argument, never returned.[3]

In 2014, another lawsuit was called for by an Egyptian writer named Ahmad al-Gamal, a columnist for *Al-Yawm Al-Sabi*. He advocated that Egypt sue Israel for damages caused by the ten biblical plagues. He said, "We want compensation for the plagues that were inflicted upon [us] as a result of the curses that the Jews' ancient forefathers [cast] upon our ancient forefathers, who did not deserve to pay for the mistake that Egypt's ruler at the time, Pharaoh, committed. ... We want compensation for the gold, silver, copper, precious stones, fabrics, hides and lumber, and for [all] animal meat, hair, hides and wool, and for other materials."[4]

Of course, the lawsuit never made it into any non-Muslim court. These ridiculous lawsuits and countless other fraudulent claims against the Jewish people expose the hypocrisy of many Muslim clerics who deny that ancient Israel even existed. Their eager willingness to agree with the lawsuits reveals that they fully know the biblical events occurred and that the Jews are the rightful owners of the land promised to them by God through Abraham.

There's certainly no need to feel bad for the ancient Egyptians who enslaved and mistreated God's people for centuries. What was taken from them did not technically belong to them because of their exploitation of the Jews. Wealth didn't belong to the Egyptians any more then it belonged to Germany after Hitler plundered the Jews of Europe and looted from them generations of their accumulated wealth, artwork, personal and family belongings, and even the gold fillings from the teeth of those who were gassed to death during the Holocaust. Theft is wrong and is a criminal act. The angelic armies are going to restore back to the church what the thief, the dirty devil, has stolen. The devil doesn't want to let go of it, but the Lord is going to shake it loose. Don't be troubled about what you hear on the news concerning global financial shaking and unstable and volatile markets. For those in the world system it's a cause for alarm, but for the people of God its reason to rejoice because we know what the shaking is all about.

> Then He said to Abram: "Know certainly that your descendants will be strangers in a land that is not theirs, and will serve them, and they will afflict them four hundred years. And also the nation whom they serve I will judge; afterward they shall come out with great possessions" (Genesis 15:13-14).

God made a covenant with Abraham that when his descendants came out of Egypt they would not go emptyhanded. Some Christians are always looking for the rapture of the church and are willing to leave emptyhanded and downtrodden. We do not find these types of negative spiritual parallels in the Scripture. Jesus died on the cross to purchase a triumphant church, not a church that is crushed in debt and financial distress, hoping to escape before things completely fall apart. We are going to be caught up in the air to meet the Lord in the clouds, but when this happens we will not be stepping off of the playing field in defeat but in total victory. The Holy Spirit is with us now, still working to lead us into financial triumph.

According to the word that I covenanted with you when you came out of Egypt, so My Spirit remains among you; do not fear! (Haggai 2:5)

God made a covenant with Abraham (in Genesis 15) that spoke of his descendants coming out of Egypt with great possessions. In the days of Haggai the prophet we see the Holy Spirit will release an end-time glory that will surpass the glory of former revivals and former financial blessings. The kingdom of Israel was at its zenith under the reign of Solomon, who established such prosperity that silver was considered to have no value.

All King Solomon's drinking vessels were gold, and all the vessels of the House of the Forest of Lebanon were pure gold. Not one was silver, for this was accounted as nothing in the days of Solomon (2 Chronicles 9:20).

The Lord is bringing the church back to the gold standard of winning in finances. The reign of Solomon was an example of where the wisdom of God can carry the church. The Holy Spirit will release the wisdom for investing, buying, selling, and other strategies to establish prosperity for the church. Angels will be sent to convey the will of God concerning what, where, when, and how to invest. As we work with the angels, we will surge into new levels of prosperity.

For thus says the Lord of hosts: "Once more (it is a little while) *I will shake heaven and earth, the sea and dry land; and I will shake all nations, and they shall come to the Desire of All Nations, and I will fill this temple with glory," says the Lord of hosts. "The silver is Mine, and the gold is Mine," says the Lord of hosts. "The glory of this latter temple shall be greater than the former," says the Lord of hosts. "And in this place I will give peace," says the Lord of hosts* (Haggai 2:6–9).

The Lord of hosts (*Jehovah Tsaba*) is going to once again shake things up. The earth and everything in it, including the silver and gold and precious metals, was all created by Him and He can do with it whatever He wants for no other reason than the fact that it's His. The whole planet is His (see Ps. 24:1). For example, I don't own your car, so I can't come over and take your keys and start driving it. But I do own my car, and if I want to drive it, sell it, or give it away to someone then I can because I'm the lawful owner. Similarly, God is going to shake things to cause movement where valuable natural resources that He owns are transferred over into the hands of His people. The silver and gold is His and He can send it to you or show you how to acquire it. How will this take place? It will transpire through the power of the Lord of hosts, *Jehovah Tsaba*, the Almighty Warrior who is the captain of the armies of heaven.

> *Arise, shine; for your light has come! And the glory of the Lord is risen upon you. For behold, the darkness shall cover the earth, and deep darkness the people; but the Lord will arise over you, and His glory will be seen upon you. The Gentiles shall come to your light, and kings to the brightness of your rising* (Isaiah 60:1–3).

There is always a parallel truth regarding the nation of Israel and the church of God. The glory of the Lord is rising upon Israel and the church in a tangible way that can be seen by the Gentiles. The glory of God consists of His goodness expressed toward you through His peace, love, joy, health, and financial prosperity. The *glory* is something that the Gentiles are able to see with their eyes. They do not understand spiritual things; they can only relate to what they see or can physically validate.

A pastor's wife shared with Kelly and me how she was the daughter of a wealthy unsaved father who owned a large car dealership.

After completing high school, this woman decided to go to a Christian Bible school that had a strong Spirit-filled emphasis. The father told her, "I do not want you going to a Bible college, especially one that is Pentecostal. If you go you will never get another penny of support from me!"

She went anyway in obedience to the call of God, and while there she rode a bicycle all over campus because she didn't have a car. She met a godly man with a calling into the ministry, and they were married upon graduating from the Bible school. They moved to a certain city and established a powerful church that soon began to spread a positive influence over the whole city as many were saved and then brought up in the faith. After several years passed by with no contact, the father decided to go and visit his daughter. He met her and her husband at the church building. After seeing the enormous church building structure and viewing the gorgeous state-of-the-art sanctuary, he was greatly perplexed. He asked, "How did you get this place?"

They responded by saying, "We had it custom built from the ground up by a large construction firm."

"But how did you pay for it?" He replied.

The daughter said, "Oh, that was easy. We simply paid cash for it. The entire facility is debt free."

The father dug deeper and asked, "But how did you do it?"

The daughter point blank said, "We did it by the power and the blessing of God." At this point the father fell to his knees and asked for her and her husband's forgiveness. While there on his knees he accepted Jesus as his Lord and Savior. The daughter personally told me that the first thing her father did when he stood up was to pull out his checkbook and write a check to be a part of the work that God was doing there. The glory of God is rising upon you and the Gentiles will *see* it.

Give no offense, either to the Jews or to the Greeks or to the
church of God (1 Corinthians 10:32).

According to the above Scripture, there are three categories
of humanity. In the Old Testament there were only two categories,
which were Jew and Gentile. During that specific dispensation you
were either a Jew, who had access to God and His blessings through
covenant privilege, or you were a Gentile who belonged to one of the
many nations of the world, all of which were separated from God and
had no covenant connection to God's redemptive plan of atonement.
In the Old Testament God clearly revealed His love for the nations of
the world, and He made provision for any Gentile to join the nation of
Israel if they rejected pagan worship and false gods. Ruth the Moabi-
tess would be a great example of someone who was formerly a Gentile
but became a Jew. Today in the New Testament there are three categories of humanity. If you are a Christian then you *are not* a Gentile;
rather, you are now in the third category of being in the church of
God. Many non-Jewish Christians still wrongly identify themselves as
Gentiles. The Gentiles are the lost unbelievers who have not received
eternal life through Christ Jesus. If you are a Christian then you are
not a Gentile.

> *Then you shall see and become radiant, and your heart*
> *shall swell with joy; because the abundance of the sea shall*
> *be turned to you, the wealth of the Gentiles shall come to*
> *you* (Isaiah 60:5).

The Lord is referring here to His glory coming upon His people
and thus accessing the wealth of the lucrative multibillion dollar sea
trading industry, in which *the abundance of the seas shall be turned to*
you. There are thousands of commercial ships that plow the oceans of
the world in the business of international trade. Perhaps you've heard
of the ship called the Emma Mærsk—its length of 1,302 feet is longer

than three football fields. The ship's enormous width makes it too wide to pass through the Panama Canal. It carries over 15,000 containers on its journey from China to England. Each trip moves over a billion dollars' worth of products. The businessmen and businesswomen in the church must be aware of global consumerism and think globally, not just locally. There will be Christians who will acquire their own ships to establish mutually profitable trade with the nation of Israel and with other countries.

> *You shall drink the milk of the Gentiles, and milk the breast of kings; you shall know that I, the Lord, am your Savior and your Redeemer, the Mighty One of Jacob* (Isaiah 60:16).

Drinking the milk of the Gentiles and their kings isn't referring to dairy milk from cows. This is a reference to their wealth and financial resources, and God is now causing it to flow to His people that they may drink it. When this happens *then you shall know* the Lord in a special way through the avenue of His redeeming power toward your finances. God has a plan to redeem you from all lack and financial struggle as you walk in His covenant financial principles and work with His angels.

> *A good man leaves an inheritance to his children's children, but the wealth of the sinner is stored up for the righteous* (Proverbs 13:22).

For countless years the sinners have been storing up wealth for the righteous. The wealth of the world is no longer static, but because of computers and other technical platforms of exchange wealth is now very dynamic and on the move 24 hours of the day. Billions of dollars of wealth are exchanged each day on the stock market, through currency trading, and through countless other mediums of exchange.

Wealth is all around you. Wealth is more than greenish looking paper currency with the pictures of old men on them from previous generations. Your wealth is a combination of those things you have accumulated, such as your clothes, your furniture, your vehicles, your tools, and even your recreational gear. God will cause many forms of wealth to be placed in your hands.

As the Old Testament age closed out and the New Testament was established through the precious blood of our Lord Jesus, we find that Jesus is the full representation and fulfillment of all that was spoken of Him from the Old Testament prophets. Because of this we don't really see the name Jehovah used in the New Testament Scriptures. For example, we don't find names such as *Jehovah-Shalom* or *Jehovah-Jireh* mentioned in the four gospels or other letters written to the churches. But there are a few exceptions to this, and one of them can be found in the book of James.

> *Come now, you rich, weep and howl for your miseries that are coming upon you! Your riches are corrupted, and your garments are moth-eaten. Your gold and silver are corroded, and their corrosion will be a witness against you and will eat your flesh like fire.* **You have heaped up treasure in the last days.** *Indeed the wages of the laborers who mowed your fields, which you kept back by fraud, cry out; and the cries of the reapers have reached the ears of the* **Lord of Sabaoth.** *You have lived on the earth in pleasure and luxury; you have fattened your hearts as in a day of slaughter. You have condemned, you have murdered the just; he does not resist you* (James 5:1–6).

Notice the Scripture says *you have heaped up treasure in the last days*. The writer James was the younger brother of Jesus, and he was the pastor of the church in Jerusalem. James reveals to us a work of

God that will unfold in the last days before the return of the Lord Jesus in which financial retribution is carried out on behalf of God's people. Who is responsible for extracting the wealth of the sinner gained by fraudulent means? James identifies the Lord of Sabaoth as the doer of this work. Who is the Lord of Sabaoth? This is a transliteration from Hebrew to Greek of the name *Jehovah Tsaba*, who is the Almighty Warrior who is the captain of the armies of heaven. In the minds of the ancient Hebrews, *Jehovah Tsaba* was the leader and commander of the armies of Israel who went with them into battle along with the angelic army to defeat the Gentile worshipers of idols and false gods. The Lord is sending His angels into battle in the spiritual realm to create financial tremors in the natural realm, which will result in God's people being supernaturally positioned to receive the reallocation of wealth as it is released.

Just as the Egyptians were spoiled of their wealth that was fraudulently gained through the cruel enslavement of the Israelites, so too will God shake the corrupt banking and corporate financial systems of this world through releasing His angelic army to go and dislodge finances and move them into the hands of God's people who are *proven financial stewards.* The unbiblical practices of fractional reserve banking (a legalized form of fraud); exorbitant interest; slush funds; complex and toxic derivatives; price fixing of stocks, commodities, and precious metals; insider trading; out-of-control greed; and many other crooked forms of cheating and scamming will be dealt with by *Jehovah Tsaba* as His angelic army shakes loose the stored up wealth.

The angels under the direction of *Jehovah Tsaba* are very powerful and able to swiftly do the work of God. I met one of these mighty angels while ministering in a conference in Taiwan. The angel was named Boaz, and he appeared to me while in a vision from God as I prayed in my hotel suite. He was about seven feet tall, and he was completely bronze in color. His body color, his hair, clothes, belt, and everything on him was bronze in color. He told me that he has been on the earth since the Bronze Age (how fitting). Ezekiel the prophet also met a heavenly being who was bronze in color.

> *He took me there, and behold, there was a man whose appearance was like the appearance of bronze* (Ezekiel 40:3).

The angel and I talked, and he shared with me that he was the leader of a division of 3,000 special angels who are assigned to bring financial provision to ministers who do the work of God upon the earth. He revealed to me that at the appointed time he would visit me in the future and cause full provision to be released for projects that God had called me to do. In the Bible we read of the story of Ruth and Boaz. It says that Boaz was a man of great wealth (see Ruth 2:1). After the vision ended I walked from my room to the conference hall because I was the next minister scheduled to speak. As I walked into the expansive conference room the entire meeting area was saturated with the glory of God. The conference host was concluding his message, and he was preaching with a compassionate anointing. To my great surprise he was pleading for the many ministers in attendance who had gathered from various countries, imploring them to allow God to bring a Boaz contributor into their lives who would be able to bring tremendous financial support to their needed projects. I could hardly believe my ears. Here he was preaching about Boaz, and I just had a visitation by an angel named Boaz.

Ministers need to expect *wealthy Boaz supporters* to be directed to their ministries by angels. This doesn't necessarily mean that the Boaz contributor sent to a minister will be a man like the Boaz who married Ruth. Throughout church history many of the greatest givers have been women—I suspect more so than men. We see an example of this in the following verse concerning the Lord's ministry.

Now it came to pass, afterward, that He went through every city and village, preaching and bringing the glad tidings of the kingdom of God. And the twelve were with Him, and certain women who had been healed of evil spirits and infirmities—Mary called Magdalene, out of whom had come seven demons, and Joanna the wife of Chuza, Herod's steward, and Susanna, and many others who provided for Him from their substance (Luke 8:1–3).

Mary Magdalene, Joanna, Susanna, and many others financially supported the Lord's ministry. While I'm sure He had many male donors, notice how it appears that His primary donors were women. The angels of God will work night and day to make divine connections for those who are called to partner with a minister of the gospel to help him or her preach the gospel around the world.

Are you ready to meet *Jehovah Tsaba* and those who are in His supernatural heavenly army? I would like to now share with you *six sharp angelic arrows to activate the end-time wealth transfer into your life.* As you implement these sharp arrows you will begin to experientially know Jesus as *Jehovah Tsaba*, the Almighty Warrior who is captain of the angelic armies.

Six Sharp Angelic Arrows to Activate the End-Time Wealth Transfer into Your Life

Arrow 1. Use your faith in God's Word to believe for *Jehovah Tsaba* to do financial miracles in your life (see Rom. 10:17). Do not passively wait for this to happen. Be aggressive with your faith and meditate on the powerful Scriptures that we examined in this chapter. Pursue God and the blessings that rightfully belong to you as a covenant child of God. Continually keep God's Word before your eyes day and night. Meditate deeply on those Scriptures that the Holy Spirit is emphasizing to you. Search the Bible for *rhema* words that quicken your spirit. This will supply you with a constant stream of faith to connect with the miracle working power of God.

Arrow 2. Worship God as *Jehovah Tsaba*. Jesus instructed us to pray by saying, "Our Father in heaven, hallowed be your name" (Matt. 6:9). To *hallow* is to sanctify and set apart the name of God. Jesus is instructing us to pray in a way that causes the name of God to be treated as holy. David said, "And those who know Your name will put their trust in You" (Ps. 9:10). The more you understand God's name, the more you will trust Him to do what His name declares Him to be and to do.

Arrow 3. Don't try to figure out how God will do it. Just live your life fully for God and relax and let Him take care of all the little details (see 1 Pet. 5:7). A dear friend of mine from out of state volunteered to remodel certain parts of our church building at no charge. He even paid for many of the new materials that were used from his own building supply store that he owns. He arrived to carry out the work by pulling up in a shiny new Ford pickup truck, which was one of Ford's most expensive, high-end models. When I asked him how he purchased his truck, he told me the following story.

There was an elderly lady who shopped in his store from time to time, making small purchases such as a light bulb or a few other small home-good items. My friend always showed Christian kindness to her and offered to help her every time she walked into his store. One day, the lady broke down and started crying in his store. Not knowing what was happening, he quickly went to see if there was anything he could do to help her. She explained that her husband of many years had died not too long ago and she missed him so much. My friend began to pray for this woman in the store, there in the busy aisle as customers walked by. The woman was greatly encouraged and left the store deeply blessed by his prayer and emotionally stabilized.

A few days later she came back to the store to thank him for his prayers. With gratitude she said, "I wish there were something I could do for you to show my appreciation for your kindness. Is there anything you want?"

My friend laughed and jokingly said, "Well, I would like a new top-of-the-line Ford pickup truck!"

The lady responded by saying, "I don't have any extra money, but my husband worked for Ford Motors for many years. I think he has some stock from the company that he never redeemed. Let me go check."

She went and checked and found out that he did indeed have some company stock—a whole lot of company stock. She redeemed the stock and gave it to my friend. It was exactly enough for him to purchase his dream truck. So, be yourself and just love God and all people sincerely, and God will take care of performing the miracles and everything else.

Arrow 4. Get comfortable with angelic encounters and their activity. Keep in mind that when God wants to do something, He doesn't push a button on a control panel. If He wants something done, then He uses His angels to do it (see Heb. 1:14). Jesus also works through us because He is the head of the church and we are the body. Your head can't do anything without your body. If you took your head off of your neck and shoulders and sat it on a table, then your head would not be able to do a single thing even if it were still alive. The head needs the body. Jesus needs the church. We are His hands and feet here in the earth. So when God needs to get things done, He often combines assignments that require both angels and His people to work together. We should anticipate working with angels.

Arrow 5. Be filled with the Holy Spirit and speak in tongues regularly, praying out the mysteries and divine secrets of God. When you speak in tongues and pray in the Spirit you unveil the mysteries of God (see 1 Cor. 14:2). As you speak in tongues for extended periods of time, you begin to access the mind of God concerning His will and plan for your life. This is one of the greatest blessings to the church. It also transports us into rest and refreshing (see Isa. 28:11-12). As you pray in the Spirit, the Lord will give you insight that will cause you to smoothly navigate your way into a place of financial peace and stability. Endeavor to pray in the Spirit every day.

Arrow 6. Obey God's financial plan for your life diligently. The message of end-time wealth transfer centers on stewardship. If you are faithful over a little, then the Lord can place you in charge over much (see Luke 16:10). But if a person is unfaithful in managing a small amount and makes mistakes there, they will only make a bigger mess if they were put in charge of a much larger amount. It is imperative that we walk in financial integrity and apply ourselves to faithfully steward what has been placed into our trust at our current level. Proven stewardship is what the Lord requires before placing kingdom resources into one's hands.

NOTES

1. Ted Olsen, "The World's Most Outrageous Biblical Lawsuit," ChristianityToday, September 1, 2003, http://www.christianitytoday.com/ct/2003/septemberweb-only/9-1-21.0.html.

2. "A Lawsuit in the Extreme?" Washington Times, September 3, 2003, http://www.washingtontimes.com/news/2003/sep/3/20030903-090203-8799r/.

3. Avi Shafran, "A Truly Historic Lawsuit," Aish.com, August 30, 2003, http://www.aish.com/jw/s/48891502.html.

4. Aron Dónzis, "Israel to Pay for 10 Plagues?" The Times of Israel, March 31, 2014, http://www.timesofisrael.com/israel-to-pay-up-for-10-plagues/.

Chapter Fifteen

SHOWING YOU HOW TO DO IT

Often when I minister somewhere I am asked afterward by other ministers how the unusual manifestations of the Spirit take place in my meetings. It reminds me of the "secret recipe" of eleven herbs and spices that Kentucky Fried Chicken uses. People want to know the recipe so they can try to cook the same type of chicken in their kitchen at home. When my family and I vacationed in Atlanta, we went to the Coca-Cola museum, which is where the secret recipe for Coke is kept in a special vault on the premises. Similarly, people are very curious about the recipe. When it comes to the manifestation of the Holy Spirit it requires what I would refer to as a *package deal*. In other words, it's not just one thing but several things that all must be put together in the right way to allow God to begin to move in a special way in a meeting. This would include and certainly not be limited to me being prepared spiritually, the hunger of the people, the location of the meeting, the preparation of the meeting to facilitate organization and planning, the level of faith that is present, and the overall will and plan of God for the specific meeting.

When we consider the manifestation of the blessings of God, we see similar characteristics. It takes more than just one single item to cause certain blessings to manifest. Some do the wrong action while hoping it will produce the right result. For example, many believers want to experience the financial prosperity of God so they can make more, save more, and thus give more money to the work of the Lord. In an effort to acquire wealth, they spend time praying, fasting, and asking God for money. But the blessing of financial empowerment does not manifest because of prayer or fasting. That statement may sound shocking to some, but it's true. A covenant of prosperity is built upon the obedience of following certain biblical principles. If you want to fly a Boeing 747 jet, you don't *pray and fast* for it to fly. Instead, you follow the *principles* that govern flight and aerodynamics. When you obey the related principles, the plane will soon get up off the ground and become airborne.

Some of the poorest people I have ever met have been prayer intercessors who loved God, prayed day and night, and at the same time lived in abject poverty with barely enough money to buy food to eat. If prayer and fasting produces wealth, then Bill Gates must pray and fast for hours every day because he is the richest man in the world at this time. But most billionaires do not pray or fast, yet they do follow biblical principles that are timeless in their effectiveness. Manifesting the blessings of God does not ride on one single component but is supported by certain timeless principles. In order to help you pull it all together and manifest the blessings of God in your life, I am going to share with you my *five proven principles for mega-manifestation.*

FIVE PROVEN PRINCIPLES FOR MEGA-MANIFESTATION.

Principle 1. Be a tither. Certain blessings you desire to see manifested can be acquired with the purchase of money. Financial blessing from God is not an entitlement, but instead it is an entrustment that you qualify for. If God cannot trust you to give back to Him 10 percent that comes to you, how could He trust you to obey Him if He gave you more? Abraham was very rich in cattle, silver, and gold. God would also like to make you very rich in stocks (or livestock if you prefer) and in precious metals. But if we want to experience the blessings of Abraham we must do the works of Abraham. Abraham was a tither before tithing was instituted in the Mosaic Law, so if we want to connect to his blessing then we should also tithe. A financial covenant is established upon trust. What is a covenant? A covenant is a spiritual contract initiated by God that is based on well-defined terms and guaranteed with an oath. If you fulfill your part then you can count on God to commit to His part of the contract.

Principle 2. Utilize the power of seed-time and harvest. If you are not a giver you will never be empowered by God to prosper financially. I have sown many gifts as seed, including rings and watches. Once I sowed a beautiful ring that I purchased while in Hamburg, Germany. The ring was very high tech and was made of a special type of ceramic that had been specially engineered. Contained within the ceramic ring were images of beautiful white horses that were running. I determined in my heart to sow the ring into the life of an anointed prophetess from central California who loved horses. Kelly and I flew to California to minister in her conference that she had invited us to minister in. I put the ring in the special box that it was purchased in and placed it in my suitcase. When we arrived at our final airport destination my suitcase came off the conveyer belt in the baggage claim area in total shreds. I've never seen anything like it even to this day. It looked like it had been clawed to pieces by a wild tiger. The airport workers had no explanation for how this could have happened. Many things had obviously fallen out, but the one thing I was fixed on finding was the ring. By the grace of God it was still there. The devil had tried to steal my seed, but he lost again. With much relief and joy I was able to present the ring to the prophetess, and she was very blessed to receive it.

Three years passed and one day while in prayer the Holy Spirit spoke to me. I heard Him just as clear as I would hear any friend speak to me. He told me to take my wife and go buy her any wedding ring she wanted. We had been married for seventeen years, and she was still wearing her grandmother's heirloom wedding ring. I had never been able to pull together the money that I wanted to get in order to buy her a really nice wedding ring. I obeyed the Spirit's directive and by faith went to a distinguished jeweler where I spent almost all of our savings on a gorgeous gold ring she picked out that was set with stunning chocolate diamonds. After spending thousands of dollars on the ring and depleting all our personal savings, the Lord swiftly followed up within five days by replenishing the account directly back to where it was before I spent the money. In essence, the Lord paid for the wedding ring. You can never out-give God. If you never plant seed in your field, then when you go to your field you will never find a harvest. Choose today to engage in the eternal principle of sowing and reaping.

Principle 3. Enlist in the night school of the Spirit and have your spiritual ears excavated. Much of our success in life can be directly linked to hearing the voice of God and being led by the Holy Spirit. Jesus attended night school in order to be taught by the heavenly Father. If Jesus needed to go to this esteemed school of higher learning, how much more do you and I also need to be in these classes? Orchestrate your life to get into these classes. Going to school at night isn't easy. It requires good planning and personal discipline. If you were going to Harvard or Yale you would have to make the sacrifice to move there, pay the expensive tuition, purchase the books and materials, and go through their demanding system of learning. Attending the night school of the Spirit is for the Christian who wants to experience God without limits. This requires you to be seriously committed to your spiritual life. There is a cost involved, but the wisdom and honors received far outweigh the cost.

Principle 4. Walk by faith and not by sight. Sounds like an easy principle, and it's often tossed around lightly as a religious cliché.

But when the storms of life blow and hope seems lost there comes a time where we must simply batten down the hatches, point the bow of the ship into the waves, and keep moving forward. The devil is a master illusionist. He tries to make you think that nothing is happening. He wants you to *feel* like God won't do it for you. But you must never confuse *faith* with *feelings*. Always stay in faith regardless of how bad the situation may look. Behind the scenes the angels of God are working to accomplish a great victory for you. Don't hinder their efforts by bawling, squalling, crying, kicking, and fussing. Stand strong in the midst of trials and difficulties and you will see turnarounds, breakthroughs, new doors open, healings, miracle favor, and much more. Be the man or woman of faith others can look to when they feel discouraged. Anytime you sense discouragement, begin to dance and praise God. By faith begin to praise Him before your blessings show up. Act like you have it now and it won't be long before you do.

Principle 5. Refuse to ever quit or give up. The U.S. Navy Seals have an understanding of what is known as the *40 percent factor*. This means that when they initially feel exhausted and they can't do another pull-up or sit-up or run another lap, they realize that in reality they are only at the 40 percent level and they actually have 60 percent left in the tank. This enables them to do things mentally and physically that are far beyond the realm of normal. I would like to suggest that you can pray a lot longer than you think you can. You can give much more than you think you can. You can live much longer than you think you can. You can accomplish much more than what you thought you could. I have seen people quit and give up just before they could have received a major, life-changing breakthrough. You must never quit. If you expend yourself and give God your best, then He will give to you His best. But if you give a halfhearted effort, God will see that and He will only respond to you in accordance with your output.

Once when ministering in northern India, I was able to share a good message and pray effectively for the many people in attendance. But I sensed that God wanted so much more to come forth out of the meeting than what we were experiencing. After my message, the conference hosts and the attendees wanted me to eat a small, personal size pizza they brought especially for me. Somehow they heard that I loved pizza, so it gave them tremendous delight to present it to me. For them to be able to find a pizza in our location seemed extraordinary. With many eyes watching me to gauge my reaction, I slowly took a big bite into the pizza. Perhaps you might be wondering what it tasted like? I would have to say it was one of the worst tasting things I've ever eaten. Not that I was ungrateful or didn't appreciate their deep love and sacrifice, but it tasted literally like eating cardboard, and that's not an overexaggeration. I took the whole pizza down in about three minutes because I was so hungry due to the frigid temperatures, but it was a real task trying to eat that cardboard pizza and smile at the same time.

The next morning I spent the entire day in prayer in preparation for the evening service. After about seven hours of fervent prayer, the Holy Spirit dropped the specific message into my heart concerning what He wanted me to share that night. He also revealed to me that He would visit the people in the night service. I poured everything into my preparation for that service. Going into that meeting I had been in constant prayer for over ten hours; I was charged from head to toe with the power of God. In the middle of my preaching the Holy Spirit fell in tremendous power. Miracles began to happen everywhere. It was the breakthrough moment in the conference that everyone had hoped for.

After ministering for over two hours, the hosts pulled me out of the clutches of the people to allow me to come aside and eat some food. They ushered me into a side room and we waited for the food to come. Other attendees also came in to eat alongside us. Everyone was eating the traditional national food that was being served. I wasn't sure what they were going to bring me, so I just relaxed and rested a bit. Then to everyone's surprise another pizza showed up that was said to be for me. It seemed that no one was quite sure of where the pizza had come from or who brought it, but they knew it was for me.

Once again, all eyes rotated over to watch Steven Brooks eat his pizza. Again, it was a small, personal size pizza, but this time it had pepperoni on it. I bit into it, and to my astonishment it tasted like I had just gone to heaven. It was absolutely incredible. I didn't rush to force it down, but I ate it slowly as they all watched and laughed because they knew I was having an epicurean moment of glory. If you give God your best, He'll always give you His best, whether it's a pizza, a home, an amazing career job, or a nation-impacting ministry. To this day I'm still not sure who brought that pizza. Maybe it was an angel. Regardless, I want to encourage you to pour out your life in the pursuit of God and in your efforts to live for Him. Push yourself. At times it won't be easy. But keep going and don't look back. As you do, you will begin to see the blessings of God manifest abundantly all around you.

CLOSING PRAYER

Heavenly Father, I pray for this precious person who has completed reading my book. I ask that from this day and onward You place a fresh anointing upon their lives to pursue You with all their strength and might. Draw them by Your Spirit into the night school classes. Release unto them new revelations of Your glory, Your majesty, Your goodness, and Your love. Let the power of Your Spirit come upon them now, clothing them with holy fire and divine glory. Let every one of their heart's desires be manifested to bring You fame and honor. Bless them, oh God, to go forth now into a life of experiencing Your very best for them. In Jesus' name I pray, amen!

Prayer to Receive Salvation in Jesus Christ and the Infilling of the Holy Spirit

Perhaps you came across this book and have not yet had the opportunity to personally receive Jesus Christ as Savior and Lord. I would like to invite you to open your heart to Him now. Please read the following verses from the Bible out loud. When you vocalize Bible verses it allows bold faith to enter into your heart.

> *Seek the Lord while He may be found, call upon Him while He is near. Let the wicked forsake his way, and the unrighteous man his thoughts; let him return to the Lord, and He will have mercy on him; and to our God, for He will abundantly pardon* (Isaiah 55:6-7).

> *All of us have become like one who is unclean, and all our righteous acts are like filthy rags; we all shrivel up like a leaf, and like the wind our sins sweep us away* (Isaiah 64:6 NIV).

> *For God so loved the world that he gave his one and only Son, that whoever believes in him shall not perish but have eternal life* (John 3:16 NIV).

> *And it shall come to pass that whoever calls on the name of the Lord shall be saved* (Acts 2:21).

> *There is salvation in no one else! God has given no other name under heaven by which we must be saved* (Acts 4:12 NLT).

> *For all have sinned and fall short of the glory of God* (Romans 3:23).

> *If you confess with your mouth, "Jesus is Lord," and believe in your heart that God raised him from the dead, you will be saved* (Romans 10:9 HCSB).

Now that you have read how you may be saved, you can obey the Word of God and make your life right with God. Simply pray the following prayer from your heart with sincerity and Jesus will give you His eternal life.

> *Dear Lord Jesus, today I choose to make You my Lord and Savior. I confess that You are the Son of God. I believe that You were raised from the dead and are alive forevermore. Because of my sin I have been separated from God, but You died on the cross and rose to life again to make it possible for me to be forgiven. While on the cross You paid the price for my sin. You have made it possible for me to now receive forgiveness of sins. Today, I choose to receive Your forgiveness and grace. Please come into my heart and forgive me of all my sins. From this moment on I surrender my life to follow You. I confess with my mouth that You are the Lord, the Son of God, and I receive You as my Lord and Savior.*

Now lift your hands and begin to praise God for saving you. From the bottom of your heart give Him thanks for saving you. Now that you belong to Jesus, allow Him to fill you to overflowing with His Holy Spirit. The following Scriptures speak of being filled with the Holy Spirit and speaking in other tongues.

> *And they were all **filled** with the Holy Spirit and began to speak with other tongues, as the Spirit gave them utterance* (Acts 2:4).

> *When Paul had laid hands on them, **the Holy Spirit came upon them**, and they spoke with tongues and prophesied* (Acts 19:6).

Now ask the heavenly Father to fill you with His Holy Spirit by praying the following prayer. "Heavenly Father, please fill me with

Your precious Holy Spirit so that I may speak in tongues and worship You all the days of my life. Let me receive the fullness of Your Spirit now."

Open your mouth and begin to speak in the new heavenly language that the Holy Spirit has given you. Let the new utterance come forth—not your own language, but the language the Holy Spirit gives you. Don't be concerned about how it sounds. It might not make sense to your mind, but it is your spirit communicating with God, and God understands everything you are speaking. Speak this out for one minute without stopping. Whenever you speak in tongues you will find that God will strengthen and refresh you.

Praise the Lord! You are now a Spirit-filled Christian on your way to heaven. Every day speak in tongues so that you will be strong in your walk with God. Now that you belong to Jesus, ask your heavenly Father to help you find a new church home so that you can grow spiritually and continue your spiritual pilgrimage toward heaven. The Holy Spirit will lead you as you search for the Christian church that God wants you to be a part of. Look for a church where you can sense the love of God and where people take a genuine interest in your spiritual growth. Seek out a church that believes the whole Bible and preaches it without compromise. And always remember *that God loves you.*

MINISTRY PARTNER INFORMATION

We would like to share with you an open invitation to partner with the life-changing ministry of Steven Brooks International. With the support of our precious *ministry partners,* Pastor Steven and Kelly are empowered to reach further into the nations of the world with God's Word and His healing touch. Working together we can experience a greater impact for the fulfillment of the Great Commission. With a world population having surpassed the staggering number of seven billion souls, the need has never been greater for anointed biblical teaching coupled with genuine manifestations of God's power to strengthen the church.

Pastor Steven's life is dedicated to the cause of ministering the bread of life to hungry souls around the world. Without the help of dedicated ministry partners, the great outreaches of this ministry would not be possible. The help of each ministry partner is vital. Whether the support is large or if it is the widow's last two pennies, every bit helps in this work. With your prayers and generous financial support we are continuing to go through the unprecedented doors of opportunity that the Lord is opening for this ministry.

Pastor Steven and Kelly absolutely treasure their ministry partners. Each ministry partner is viewed as a special gift from God and is to be highly valued. Pastor Steven and Kelly believe in covenant relationships and understand the emphasis and blessing that God places upon such divine connections. In this end-time hour God is joining those with like hearts to stand together in this sacred work. Thank you for prayerfully considering becoming a ministry partner. We encourage you to take the step and join this exciting and rewarding journey with us. Together we can make an eternal difference in the lives of precious souls, enabling us to have an expectancy to hear the Lord's voice on that blessed day, saying, "Well done, good and faithful servant."

As a ministry partner, your undertaking is to pray for Pastor Steven, his family, and his ministry on a regular basis and support his ministry with a monthly financial contribution.

As a ministry partner, you will receive the following benefits.

- Impartation that is upon Pastor Steven's life to be upon you to help you accomplish what God has called you to do

- Consistent prayer for you by Pastor Steven

- Regular ministry partner newsletter to build your faith and feed your spirit

- Mutual faith in God for His best return on all your giving

- Eternal share in the heavenly rewards obtained through this ministry

Become a ministry partner now!

Name _____

Address _____

Phone Number _____

E-mail Address _____

_____ Yes, Pastor Steven, I join with you in ministry partnership and I (we) stand with you as you continue to preach the gospel to all the earth.

Please mail your information to:

Steven Brooks International
PO Box 3456
Mooresville, NC 28117

You may also become a ministry partner by registering at our online Web site at: www.stevenbrooks.org. Once there, please click on the "partner" link to sign up.

For booking information and upcoming meetings regarding Steven Brooks International please visit our Web site at: www.stevenbrooks .org or e-mail us at: info@stevenbrooks.org.

ABOUT STEVEN BROOKS

Steven Brooks is known worldwide for his outstanding ability to preach and teach the Word of God with refreshing clarity and spiritual precision. His powerful healing and miracle ministry have taken him throughout America and around the globe with confirming signs and wonders that infuse the believer with bold faith and vivacious joy in Christ.

The ministry of Steven and Kelly Brooks continues to reach multitudes of souls around the world. Steven is widely known for his ability to teach God's Word in a clear and understandable way to new believers as well as to those who have been in the faith for decades. He operates fluently in the gifts of the Holy Spirit and tremendous miracles take place when he prays. Steven stresses the importance of faith in God and the eternal value of living a life of daily prayer and deep devotion to the Lord. His heart is to see the lost saved and the church strengthened. He is used by the Lord as an end-time servant to prepare God's people for global revival and an unprecedented outpouring of God's Spirit upon the earth.